MACMILLAN MASTER GUIDES

GENERAL EDITOR: JAMES GIBSON

Published

JANE AUSTEN	*Emma* Norman Page
	Sense and Sensibility Judy Simons
	Persuasion Judy Simons
	Pride and Prejudice Raymond Wil...
	Mansfiel...
SAMUEL BECKETT	*Waiting f...*
WILLIAM BLAKE	*Songs of ...*
	Experi...
ROBERT BOLT	*A Man fo...*
EMILY BRONTË	*Wuthering ... ... D. Spear*
GEOFFREY CHAUCER	*The Miller's Tale* Michael Alexander
	The Pardoner's Tale Geoffrey Lester
	The Wife of Bath's Tale Nicholas Marsh
	The Knight's Tale Anne Samson
	The Prologue to the Canterbury Tales
	Nigel Thomas and Richard Swan
JOSEPH CONRAD	*The Secret Agent* Andrew Mayne
CHARLES DICKENS	*Bleak House* Dennis Butts
	Great Expectations Dennis Butts
	Hard Times Norman Page
GEORGE ELIOT	*Middlemarch* Graham Handley
	Silas Marner Graham Handley
	The Mill on the Floss Helen Wheeler
HENRY FIELDING	*Joseph Andrews* Trevor Johnson
E. M. FORSTER	*Howards End* Ian Milligan
	A Passage to India Hilda D. Spear
WILLIAM GOLDING	*The Spire* Rosemary Sumner
	Lord of the Flies Raymond Wilson
OLIVER GOLDSMITH	*She Stoops to Conquer* Paul Ranger
THOMAS HARDY	*The Mayor of Casterbridge* Ray Evans
	Tess of the d'Urbervilles James Gibson
	Far from the Madding Crowd Colin
	Temblett-Wood
JOHN KEATS	*Selected Poems* John Garrett
PHILIP LARKIN	*The Whitsun Weddings* and *The Less*
	Deceived Andrew Swarbrick
D. H. LAWRENCE	*Sons and Lovers* R. P. Draper
HARPER LEE	*To Kill a Mockingbird* Jean Armstrong
GERARD MANLEY HOPKINS	*Selected Poems* R. J. C. Watt
CHRISTOPHER MARLOWE	*Doctor Faustus* David A. Male
VIRGINIA WOOLF	*To the Lighthouse* John Mepham
THE METAPHYSICAL POETS	Joan van Emden

MACMILLAN MASTER GUIDES

THOMAS MIDDLETON and WILLIAM ROWLEY	*The Changeling* Tony Bromham
ARTHUR MILLER	*The Crucible* Leonard Smith *Death of a Salesman* Peter Spalding
GEORGE ORWELL	*Animal Farm* Jean Armstrong
WILLIAM SHAKESPEARE	*Richard II* Charles Barber *Hamlet* Jean Brooks *King Lear* Francis Casey *Henry V* Peter Davison *The Winter's Tale* Diana Devlin *Julius Caesar* David Elloway *Macbeth* David Elloway *Measure for Measure* Mark Lilly *Henry IV Part I* Helen Morris *Romeo and Juliet* Helen Morris *The Tempest* Kenneth Pickering *A Midsummer Night's Dream* Kenneth Pickering *Coriolanus* Gordon Williams *Antony and Cleopatra* Martin Wine
GEORGE BERNARD SHAW	*St Joan* Leonée Ormond
RICHARD SHERIDAN	*The School for Scandal* Paul Ranger *The Rivals* Jeremy Rowe
ALFRED TENNYSON	*In Memoriam* Richard Gill
ANTHONY TROLLOPE	*Barchester Towers* Ken Newton
JOHN WEBSTER	*The White Devil* and *The Duchess of Malfi* David A. Male

Forthcoming

CHARLOTTE BRONTË	*Jane Eyre* Robert Miles
JOHN BUNYAN	*The Pilgrim's Progress* Beatrice Batson
T. S. ELIOT	*Murder in the Cathedral* Paul Lapworth *Selected Poems* Andrew Swarbrick
BEN JONSON	*Volpone* Michael Stout
RUDYARD KIPLING	*Kim* Leonée Ormond
JOHN MILTON	*Comus* Tom Healy
WILLIAM SHAKESPEARE	*Othello* Tony Bromham *As You Like It* Kiernan Ryan
VIRGINIA WOOLF	*Mrs Dalloway* Julian Pattison
W. B. YEATS	*Selected Poems* Stan Smith

MACMILLAN MASTER GUIDES
CORIOLANUS
BY WILLIAM SHAKESPEARE

GORDON WILLIAMS

with an Introduction by
HAROLD BROOKS

MACMILLAN
EDUCATION

First edition 1987

Published by
MACMILLAN EDUCATION LTD
Houndmills, Basingstoke, Hampshire RG21 2XS
and London
Companies and representatives
throughout the world

Typeset by TecSet Ltd, Wallington, Surrey

Printed in Hong Kong

British Library Cataloguing in Publication Data
Williams, Gordon, 1935 —
Coriolanus by William Shakespeare. —
(Macmillan master guides)
1. Shakespeare, William — Coriolanus
I. Title
822.3'3   PR2805
ISBN 0–333–43281–9Pbk
ISBN 0–333–43282–7 Pbk export

CONTENTS

GENERAL EDITOR'S PREFACE

The aim of the Macmillan Master Guides is to help you to appreciate the book you are studying by providing information about it and by suggesting ways of reading and thinking about it which will lead to a fuller understanding. The section on the writer's life and background has been designed to illustrate those aspects of the writer's life which have influenced the work, and to place it in its personal and literary context. The summaries and critical commentary are of special importance in that each brief summary of the action is followed by an examination of the significant critical points. The space which might have been given to repetitive explanatory notes has been devoted to a detailed analysis of the kind of passage which might confront you in an examination. Literary criticism is concerned with both the broader aspects of the work being studied and with its detail. The ideas which meet us in reading a great work of literature, and their relevance to us today, are an essential part of our study, and our Guides look at the thought of their subject in some detail. But just as essential is the craft with which the writer has constructed his work of art, and this may be considered under several technical headings – characterisation, language, style and stagecraft, for example.

The authors of these Guides are all teachers and writers of wide experience, and they have chosen to write about books they admire and know well in the belief that they can communicate their admiration to you. But you yourself must read and know intimately the book you are studying. No one can do that for you. You should see this book as a lamp-post. Use it to shed light, not to lean against. If you know your text and know what it is saying about life, and how it says it, then you will enjoy it, and there is no better way of passing an examination in literature.

JAMES GIBSON

AN INTRODUCTION TO THE STUDY OF SHAKESPEARE'S PLAYS

A play as a work of art exists to the full only when performed. It must hold the audience's attention throughout the performance, and, unlike a novel, it can't be put down and taken up again. It is important to experience the play as if you are seeing it on the stage for the first time, and you should begin by reading it straight through. Shakespeare builds a play in dramatic units which may be divided into smaller subdivisions, or episodes, marked off by exits and entrances and lasting as long as the same actors are on the stage. Study it unit by unit.

The first unit provides the exposition which is designed to put the audience into the picture. In the second unit we see the forward movement of the play as one situation changes into another. The last unit in a tragedy or a tragical play will bring the catastrophe and in comedy — and some of the history plays — an unravelling of the complications, what is called a *dénouement*.

The onward movement of the play from start to finish is its progressive structure. We see the chain of cause and effect (the plot) and the progressive revelation and development of character. The people, their characters and their motives drive the plot forward in a series of scenes which are carefully planned to give variety of pace and excitement. We notice fast-moving and slower-moving episodes, tension mounting and slackening, and alternate fear and hope for the characters we favour. Full-stage scenes, such as stately councils and processions or turbulent mobs, contrast with scenes of small groups or even single speakers. Each of the scenes presents a deed or event which changes the situation. In performances, entrances and exits and stage actions are physical facts, with more impact than on the page. That impact Shakespeare relied upon, and we must restore it by an effort of the imagination.

Shakespeare's language is just as diverse. Quickfire dialogue is followed by long speeches, and verse changes to prose. There is a wide range of speech — formal, colloquial, dialect, 'Mummerset' and the broken English of foreigners, for example. Songs, instrumental music, and the noise of battle, revelry and tempest, all extend the range of dramatic expression. The dramatic use of language is enhanced by skilful stagecraft, by costumes, by properties such as beds, swords and Yorick's skull, by such stage business as kneeling, embracing and giving money, and by use of such features of the stage structure as the balcony and the trapdoor.

By these means Shakespeare's people are brought vividly to life and cleverly individualised. But though they have much to tell us about human nature, we must never forget that they are characters in a play, not in real life. And remember, they exist to enact the play, not the play to portray *them*.

Shakespeare groups his characters so that they form a pattern, and it is useful to draw a diagram showing this. Sometimes a linking character has dealings with each group. The pattern of persons belongs to the symmetric structure of the play, and its dramatic unity is reinforced and enriched by a pattern of resemblances and contrasts; for instance, between characters, scenes, recurrent kinds of imagery, and words. It is not enough just to notice a feature that belongs to the symmetric structure, you should ask what its relevance is to the play as a whole and to the play's ideas.

These ideas and the dramatising of them in a central theme, or several related to each other, are a principal source of the dramatic unity. In order to see what themes are present and important, look, as before, for pattern. Observe the place in it of the leading character. In tragedy this will be the protagonist, in comedy heroes and heroines, together with those in conflict or contrast with them. In *Henry IV Part I,* Prince Hal is being educated for kingship and has a correct estimate of honour, while Falstaff despises honour, and Hotspur makes an idol of it. Pick out the episodes of great intensity as, for example, in *King Lear* where the theme of spiritual blindness is objectified in the blinding of Gloucester, and similarly, note the emphases given by dramatic poetry as in Prospero's 'Our revels now are ended . . .' or unforgettable utterances such as Lear's 'Is there any cause in Nature that makes these hard hearts?' Striking stage-pictures such as that of Hamlet behind the King at prayer will point to leading themes, as will all the parallels and recurrences, including those of phrase and imagery. See whether, in the play you are studying, themes known to be favourites with Shakespeare are prominent, themes such as those of order and disorder, relationships disrupted by mistakes about identity, and appearance and reality. The latter were bound to fascinate Shakespeare, whose theatrical art worked by means of illusions which pointed beyond the surface of actual life to underlying truths. In looking at themes beware of attempts to make the play fit some orthodoxy a critic believes in — Freudian perhaps, or Marxist, or dogmatic Christian theology — and remember that its ideas, though they often have a bearing on ours, are Elizabethan.

Some of Shakespeare's greatness lies in the good parts he wrote for the actors. In his demands upon them, and the opportunities he provided, he bore their professional skills in mind and made use of their physical prowess, relished by a public accustomed to judge fencing and wrestling as expertly as we today judge football and tennis. As a member of the professional group of players called the Chamberlain's Men he knew each actor he was writing for. To play his women he had highly trained boys. As paired heroines they were often contrasted, short with tall, for example, or one vivacious and enterprising, the other more conventionally feminine.

Richard Burbage, the company's leading man, was famous as a great tragic actor, and he took leading roles in seven of Shakespeare's *tragedies*. Though each of the seven has its own distinctiveness, we shall find at the centre of all of them a tragic protagonist possessing tragic greatness, not just one 'tragic flaw' but a tragic vulnerability. He will have a character which makes him unfit to cope with the tragic situations confronting him, so that his tragic errors bring down upon him tragic suffering and finally a tragic catastrophe. Normally, both the suffering and the catastrophe are far worse than he can be said to deserve, and others are engulfed in them who deserve such a fate less or not at all. Tragic terror is aroused in us because, though exceptional, he is sufficiently near to normal humankind for his fate to remind us of what can happen to human beings like ourselves, and because we see in it a combination of inexorable law and painful mystery. We recognise the principle of cause and effect where in a tragic world errors return upon those who make them, but we are also aware of the tragic disproportion between cause and effect. In a tragic world you may kick a stone and start an avalanche which will destroy you and others with you. Tragic pity is aroused in us by this disproportionate suffering, and also by all the kinds of suffering undergone by every character who has won our imaginative sympathy. Imaginative sympathy is wider than moral approval, and is felt even if suffering does seem a just and logical outcome. In addition to pity and terror we have a sense of tragic waste because catastrophe has affected so much that was great and fine. Yet we feel also a tragic exaltation. To our grief the men and women who represented those values have been destroyed, but the values themselves have been shown not to depend upon success, nor upon immunity from the worst of tragic sufferings and disaster.

Comedies have been of two main kinds, or cross-bred from the two. In critical comedies the governing aim is to bring out the absurdity or irrationality of follies and abuses, and make us laugh at them. Shakespeare's comedies often do this, but most of them belong primarily to the other kind – romantic comedy. Part of the romantic appeal is to our liking for suspense; they are dramas of averted threat, beginning in trouble and ending in joy. They appeal to the romantic senses of adventure and of wonder, and to complain that they are improbable is silly because the improbability, the marvellousness, is part of the pleasure. They dramatise stories of romantic love, accompanied by love doctrine – ideas and ideals of love. But they are plays in two tones, they are comic as well as romantic. There is often something to laugh at even in the love stories of the nobility and gentry, and just as there is high comedy in such incidents as the cross-purposes of the young Athenians in the wood, and Rosalind as 'Ganymede' teasing Orlando, there is always broad comedy for character of lower rank. Even where one of the sub-plots has no effect on the main plot, it may take up a topic from it and present it in a more comic way.

What is there in the play to make us laugh or smile? We can distinguish many kinds of comedy it may employ. *Language* can amuse by its wit, or by absurdity, as in Bottom's malapropisms. Feste's nonsense-phrases, so fatuously admired by Sir Andrew, are deliberate, while his catechising of Olivia is clown-routine. Ass-headed Bottom embraced by the Fairy Queen is a *comic spectacle* combining costume and stage-business. His wanting to play every part is *comedy of character*. Phebe disdaining Silvius and in love with 'Ganymede', or Malvolio treating Olivia as though she had written him a love-letter is *comedy of situation*; the situation is laughably different from what Phebe or Malvolio supposes. A comic let-down or anticlimax can be devastating, as we see when Aragon, sure that he deserves Portia, chooses the silver casket only to find the portrait not of her but of a 'blinking idiot'. By *slapstick, caricature* or sheer *ridiculousness of situation*, comedy can be exaggerated into farce, which Shakespeare knows how to use on occasion. At the opposite extreme, before he averts the threat, he can carry it to the brink of tragedy, but always under control.

Dramatic irony is the result of a character or the audience anticipating an outcome which, comically or tragically, turns out very differently. Sometimes *we* foresee that it will. The speaker never foresees how ironical, looking back, the words or expectations will appear. When she says, 'A little water clears us of this deed' Lady Macbeth has no prevision of her sleep-walking words, 'Will these hands ne'er be clean?' There is irony in the way in which in all Shakespeare's tragic plays except *Richard II* comedy is found in the very heart of the tragedy. The Porter scene in *Macbeth* comes straight after Duncan's murder. In *Hamlet* and *Antony and Cleopatra* comic episodes lead into the catastrophe: the rustic Countryman brings Cleopatra the means of death, and the satirised Osric departs with Hamlet's assent to the fatal fencing match. The Porter, the Countryman and Osric are not mere 'comic relief', they contrast with the tragedy in a way that adds something to it, and affects our response.

A sense of the comic and the tragic is common ground between Shakespeare and his audience. Understandings shared with the audience are necessary to all drama. They include conventions, i.e. assumptions, contrary to what factual realism would demand, which the audience silently agrees to accept. It is, after all, by a convention, what Coleridge called a 'willing suspension of disbelief', that an actor is accepted as Hamlet. We should let a play teach us the conventions it depends on. Shakespeare's conventions allow him to take a good many liberties, and he never troubles about inconsistencies that wouldn't trouble an audience. What matters to the dramatist is the effect he creates. So long as we are responding as he would wish. Shakespeare would not care whether we could say by what means he has made us do so. But to appreciate his skill, and get a fuller understanding of his play, we have to distinguish these means, and find terms to describe them.

If you approach the Shakespeare play you are studying bearing in mind what is said to you here, then you will respond to it more fully than before. Yet like all works of artistic genius, Shakespeare's can only be analysed so far. His drama and its poetry will always have about them something 'which into words no critic can digest'.

HAROLD BROOKS

ACKNOWLEDGEMENTS

All references and quotations follow Philip Brockbank's edition of *Coriolanus*, the Arden Shakespeare (London: Methuen, 1976).

Cover illustration: *Presentation of Darius's Family to Alexander* by Paolo Veronese. Photograph © National Gallery, London

The drawing of the Globe Theatre is by courtesy of Alec Pearson.

1 SHAKESPEARE'S LIFE

AND

CAREER

Our knowledge of Shakespeare's life, outside the evidence of his published works, is scanty. A scattering of official documents provides us with some basic details, meagrely filled out by a few contemporaries who mention him. We have a large number of stories attaching to him, one or two of which may have a factual basis, though hardly any can be traced back to his lifetime. Most have obviously been fabricated to supply a biography where one is virtually non-existent.

Of this legendary material, perhaps the story most likely to reflect some actual event is that which is most frequently derided. Deer-poaching *may* have been one of the young Shakespeare's activities.

Certainly not all of his behaviour accorded with the most approved social standards. He married Anne Hathaway in 1582, when she was several months pregnant. This much is fact, though other accounts of sexual peccadilloes may not be. Thus a diarist noted in 1602 that Shakespeare had successfully cut in on one of the actor Burbage's lady-friends. Decades later, the poet-dramatist Davenant claimed to be Shakespeare's natural son, product of an illicit liaison between Shakespeare and his hostess at an Oxford inn. Some have sought to lend colour to such stories by reference to Shakespeare's willing to his wife the second-best bed. But such a disposition is hardly evidence of an unhappy marriage.

However, if we try to search out a picture of Shakespearean respectability, that proves another dead end. All that can be safely said is that he was born into thoroughly respectable yeoman stock. His father became a worker in soft leather, retailing his own goods. Success was affirmed when he married a prosperous farmer's daughter. So by the time of Shakespeare's birth, in April 1564, the family was thriving. He was the third of eight children, several of whom died in infancy. His father was a member of the town council and the next year was to become an alderman. The peak of his career was between 1568 and 1571 when he served as High Bailiff, or mayor, of Stratford. But a few years later the family fortunes went into decline, part of a general economic recession. In such circumstances, a spot of poaching by the eldest son might not seem such an outlandish possibility.

Elizabethan Stratford was a small market town. But at this date few towns were anything more. It was significant enough to receive intermittent visits from London theatrical troupes. These may have whetted the young Shakespeare's appetite, but the circumstances of his departure from Stratford are unknown. He left during the period between 1585 and 1592 known to biographers as 'the lost years'. Virtually nothing can be gleaned about Shakespeare's activities from 1585, when his wife delivered him twins, until 1592, when he had become sufficiently established in the London theatre world to arouse the ire of fellow-writer Robert Greene.

One thing we may confidently assume is that Shakespeare was solidly educated. His father's social status entitled him to send his children to the local grammar school free of charge. Ben Jonson's celebrated reference to Shakespeare's 'small Latine' is relative. What appeared 'small Latine' to a heavyweight like Jonson would probably equip the present-day Classics graduate.

That Shakespeare's education was backed by wit, intelligence and breadth of sympathy is abundantly demonstrated by his writings. Presumably, too, he had presence and personality, in view of his successful acting career. His versatility extended to both comedy and tragedy. He is known to have played in Jonsonian comedy, though the only specific role which can be assigned to him with confidence is that of the Ghost in *Hamlet*.

But acting is a precarious career; and the Elizabethan playwright was a company drudge. Although Shakespeare quickly established himself as leading writer for the foremost theatre company in London, the Lord Chamberlain's men, he showed shrewd business sense by investing in the company. As one of a small group of shareholders, he was able to reap the financial rewards of a success to which his own plays had contributed significantly.

The great plague of 1592–4 played havoc with the London theatres, and Shakespeare turned his hand to two neo-Ovidian narratives, *Venus and Adonis* and *The Rape of Lucrece*. In 1594 the Lord Chamberlain's company was reorganised and Shakespeare began his long association with it. At the end of 1598, after some problems with accommodation, the company moved from Shoreditch across the river to Bankside. There they built the finest theatre London had seen until then, the Globe.

Henry V and *Twelfth Night* would have been amongst the earliest Shakespearean plays given there. But it was the Globe which saw that extension of Shakespeare's range in which comedy becomes pushed in the direction of tragedy. It also saw the development of the great tragedies themselves, and the Roman plays. It is likely that the company had opened their more intimate, or private, theatre by the time that *Coriolanus* was written. It has been suggested that it was intended for performance there. But the many scenes of riot and battle would have been more effectively played on the Globe's spacious platform.

Shakespeare's late plays were designed for the private theatre. He was soon to retire to Stratford where he had maintained family and property ties throughout his London career. Nor did his theatrical interests cease then. Always the innovator, he seems finally to have found another fresh direction in collaboration, linking his genius to that of the rising star John Fletcher.

Shakespeare died on 23 April 1616 and was buried, as a man of property, in the chancel of Holy Trinity Church, Stratford.

2 TEXT AND SOURCES

2.1 TEXT

There are two ways in which I wish to consider text: I want to define the nature of a play-text and to look briefly at the means by which the printed text has been made available to us.

The actor's text
The play-text, with which this book largely deals, is a very incomplete thing. It is a part of a whole which can only be realised on stage. In the case of Shakespeare, just how much of a part the text constitutes has been subject to much debate. Charles Lamb and others, at the beginning of the nineteenth century, preferred to rest on the text and forget about theatrical realisations. In Hazlitt's words, 'Poetry and the stage do not agree well together'. Critics today, even as they remind us that Shakespeare's texts were written for the theatre, reveal in the very formulation a bias towards the written word.

It so happens that Shakespeare's texts are very fully written. Language, as well as being a medium, is often – in its deceptions and ambiguities – a thematic issue in his plays. Other playwrights may work differently, relying heavily on gesture, movement and spectacle for meaning without the same extensive linguistic underpinning. This does not make the results inferior. The mime-play, which eschews language altogether, is not a trivial branch of theatre. Shakespeare himself shows interest in it, though not in the present play. Similarly, the silent cinema is different from, but not inferior to, sound cinema. Indeed, the very phrase 'silent cinema' is an absurd misnomer, since the form relies heavily on sound – music, not speech – for emotional impact and other dramatic effects.

But Shakespeare's dramatic meanings, too, depend on the orchestration of a whole variety of elements: music, spectacle, business, line-delivery – including pauses, coughs, belches – and, of course, a whole vocabulary of gesture which, firmly established in his day, is still residually present on the modern stage. We are particularly conscious of this dependence in *Coriolanus*, which leaves more between the lines than is customary in Shakespeare. As Harley Granville-Barker (1947) puts it, much is kept inexplicit 'for the actors to develop, or elucidate in their acting', thereby making more demands on them and allowing them more opportunities (*Preface to Coriolanus*, p. 180).

That still leaves the key factor of playing to an audience. What the actor projects outwards he needs to feel bouncing back from a responsive audience. The play's effect, and consequently its meaning, depends on that audience participation. Amongst other things, a poor audience will compel the performers to go more quickly and superficially through their material than would otherwise be the case. An alertly responsive audience will detect, and so help to clarify, half-realised effects and meanings, assisting the actor towards improved emphases in subsequent performances. These give-and-take possibilities are of prime importance.

A play-text is an anomaly since it masquerades as a literary text whilst being intended for oral performance. The latter aspect makes it analogous to popular poetry in that it takes colour from the audience assembled to listen to it. Thus, if a scene or passage seems no longer to play well, the producer will feel free to adapt or cut it. On the other hand, Shakespeare's scripts have been fixed in print, and his special position as cultural hero has rendered them sacrosanct.

Historical accuracy is the proper concern of the scholar, just as communication and entertainment are that of actor or director. There are those like Granville-Barker who have made impressive efforts to bridge the gap. That this is not completely possible should matter little if respect is maintained on both sides. For each has much to learn from the other.

The scholar's text
What the textual scholar seeks to do is to establish as authentic a version of a play or poem as possible. So, in so far as we consider it better to assess Shakespeare on the basis of a reliable text rather than an unreliable one, his work is of value.

Half of Shakespeare's plays had to await the publication of a posthumous collected edition, the Folio of 1623, for their first appearance in print. *Coriolanus*, like the other Roman plays *Julius Caesar* and *Antony and Cleopatra*, was never published separately, so the 1623 Folio text is the only authoritative one. This both simplifies and complicates the editor's task. It is simplified because there can be no wavering between the reading of one authority and another. It is complicated because, where misprints or other corruptions are recognised or suspected, there can be no recourse to another text for clarification.

There was a tendency in these early editions for lines to be crowded together on a page in order to save space, or conversely to be spread out in order to fill a page. Thus lines of prose might have the appearance of poetry, and vice versa. This can be a problem when the writer is moving as fluidly between poetry and prose as Shakespeare does in *Coriolanus*.

But light may be shed on these and other difficulties by modern techniques which make it possible to distinguish the work of different compositors in the original setting up of the printed text. Each compositor is apt to have his own idosyncrasies which, once identified, may provide a key to correct emendation.

Stage directions and assignment of speeches can go awry for a variety of reasons. Confusion is especially likely in cases of unnamed characters such as the Roman citizens or Volscian conspirators. We need to know not only who is saying what, but also who is present on stage (perhaps silently) at any given moment. So entry and exit directions need to be accurate.

Coriolanus has its share of misprints, some of them more readily spotted than others. A brief sample will suggest what editors have been up against. The 1623 Folio 'scale't' is normally replaced by 'stale't' (I.i.91), 'Calves' by 'Cato's' (I.iv.57), 'hours' by 'honours' (I.v.4), 'upheld' by 'beheld' (I.ix.40), 'beesome' by 'bisson' (II.i.63), 'pray' by 'prate' (V.iii.48), 'clock'd' by 'cluck'd' (V.iii.163). 'Overture' has been replaced by 'ovator' (I.ix.46), but this one is still doubtful.

Occasionally misprints were put right in the second edition of the Folio. Thus 'wadg'd' was emended to 'wedged' (II.iii.28) and 'higher' to 'hire' (II.iii.113). But the recognition of something amiss with 'taintingly' (I.i.109) only resulted in 'tantingly'. The correct 'tauntingly' was arrived at only in the fourth edition of 1685.

An interesting instance is provided by the first Folio's 'wolvish tongue', where 'tongue' is evidently a compositor's attempt to rationalise the unfamiliar word 'toge' (II.iii.114). In the second edition, this was recognised as incorrect, but a further rationalisation yielded 'wolvish gown'. This was one of those disputed readings still worrying nineteenth-century Shakespeareans like Coleridge. But ninety per cent of the cruxes had been settled by the end of the eighteenth century, a century in which the first really scholarly editions of Shakespeare had been produced.

While act divisions are observed in the first Folio, scene divisions are an eighteenth-century innovation. They function conveniently as a mode of reference, but we should not be tyrannised by them into forgetting the fluidity of Shakespearean staging. Finicking attempts to locate the scene should also be subject to the same caution.

Philip Brockbank, in the Introduction to his Arden edition of *Coriolanus*, notes how several of the play's stage directions are 'ironic and politically expressive', resulting in one case – '*Enter* SICINIUS VELUTUS, JUNIUS BRUTUS; COMINIUS, TITUS LARTIUS, *with other Senators*' (I.i.225) – where eighteenth-century scholars, and indeed 'the class-conscious editorial majority, recast to keep the tribunes in the rear'. Clearly the point here is to emphasise the new ascendancy achieved by the people's representatives.

In short, when we look at our clean modern copies of *Coriolanus*, it is as well to bear in mind the vicissitudes undergone by Shakespeare's text over the centuries, and the way that it is being mediated to us by an editor whose prejudices we might not share.

2.2 SOURCES

The main source for Shakespeare's trilogy of Roman plays is Plutarch's *Lives of the Noble Grecians and Romans*. Plutarch was a Greek historian living in the time of Nero, the first century of the Christian era. His *Lives* was one of the great and influential books in the Renaissance, continually ransacked by poets and painters. It had been translated into French by Bishop Jacques Amyot, a fine scholar and stylist, and it was upon this translation that the English version of 1579 was based. This latter, the one used by Shakespeare, was by Thomas North, who provides a more rough-hewn prose than Amyot. But he has a vigour which clearly appealed to Shakespeare, since many of his phrases are absorbed direct into the text of *Coriolanus*.

Shakespeare may have had other ancient authors in view when writing his play. Livy's Roman history, *Ab Urbe Condita*, had served him for *The Rape of Lucrece* (1594), and it was now still more accessible through the translation of Philemon Holland (1600). Aristotle's *Politics*, too – written in Athens during the fourth century BC and available from 1598 in English translation – may have furnished certain ideas, such as those on the city or mixed government.

But Plutarch remains the decisive influence, and critics of the play have properly kept him in view. We are able to gain valuable insight into Shakespeare's methods and approach by considering what he kept and what he omitted, where his interpretations coincide with Plutarch's and where they depart.

A few indications must suffice here. In particular, the secondary characters have been much developed. Menenius is presented by Plutarch as a mediator between plebs and patricians, and delivers his belly-fable. But he dies soon after without even the means to pay for his funeral. Likewise, the role of Tullus (Aufidius) is much expanded: he only appears in Plutarch after Coriolanus's banishment. It was Shakespeare's idea to develop the relationship into a long-standing rivalry.

The two Tribunes are taken over from Plutarch, but are no longer mere cyphers of subversion. Likewise, it is only in Shakespeare that we become aware of the people as a collection of individuals. Shakespeare is interested in people at all social levels. Not only in Rome, but also in the house of Aufidius, the lower orders take on a new vitality. Coriolanus's faintly surreal discourse with the manservants at the start of IV.v is pure Shakespeare, as is the serio-comic exchange between the servants at the end.

Shakespeare's development of the women characters is crucial. The embassy of women (V.iii) derives from Plutarch, and so do elements of the special relationship between Coriolanus and his mother. But the scene with the women in Coriolanus's home (I.iii) is a major innovation, and so is Volumnia's pushing Coriolanus towards a consulship. Plutarch's Coriolanus needs no pushing in the way of political ambition. He becomes intent not on destroying Rome but on using the Volscian aristocracy to restore patrician power in Rome and thereby recover his own. Harry Levin (*Shakespeare and the Revolution of the Times*, p. 189) suggests that he was perhaps 'a half-legendary embodiment of patrician resistance to the increasing demands of the plebeians'. Shakespeare, on the other hand, opts for a more personal confrontation: Coriolanus's prideful desire for vengeance against his natural feeling for family.

One curious feature is the way in which Plutarch begins – the issue is clearly of prime importance to him – by ascribing Coriolanus's character defects to the loss of his father when he was small. Shakespeare confronts us with something of the sort, obliging us to consider connections between Volumnia's particular brand of maternal influence and Coriolanus's species of self-absorption in which the sexual and martial impulses easily elide. Yet he avoids Plutarch's directness, making no mention of Coriolanus's father – dead or otherwise. The omission is worth pondering.

3 SUMMARY
AND COMMENTARY

ACT I

Summary
The play opens with a food riot in Rome, which achieves some modest governmental reform. The patrician Menenius seeks to pacify the rioters, but another, Martius, favours violent confrontation. However, allowing the plebs to have government representation in the shape of five Tribunes lowers the temperature somewhat; and the vestigial violence is diverted to an outside enemy, the Volsces. Martius's eagerness for combat and the chance of glory is endorsed by his mother, Volumnia, though his wife has misgivings. But his marvellous exploits against the Volsces and their general, Aufidius, include the capture of an important city, Corioli. In recognition he is granted the name Coriolanus.

Act I, Scene i

Action begins noisily with a civil disturbance, prompted by a food shortage. The citizenry is 'resolved rather to die than to famish'. As frequently happens, an individual is identified as the source of the trouble. In this instance the ritual object of hatred is Caius Martius; no perverse choice, given the contempt which he reveals for the common people later on. The problem reduces to: 'Let us kill him, and we'll have corn at our own price' (9–10). But the tensions exhibited in this opening scene extend beyond the immediate problem of food shortages. There is the rift between patricians and plebs – quibbles on poor (= inferior as well as impoverished) and good (= morally as well as financially sound) showing that the citizens are astutely aware of patrician evaluations (14–15). In this same speech, too, the First Citizen notes not only how the well-to-do are too niggardly to relieve the poor, but how they wish to preserve poverty as a means of emphasising their own affluence.

What Shakespeare shows us here is not just that empty bellies are prime movers to revolt. Other conditions have to be satisfied first. The unprivileged must be prodded out of their inertia by necessity, whereupon they will be apt to start pondering their role in the social structure. But Brecht, in his 'Study of the First Scene of Shakespeare's "Coriolanus"' (p.252), properly emphasises 'how hard it is for the oppressed to become united'. Their misery will unite them once they have identified their oppressors. 'But otherwise their misery is liable to cut them off from one another, for they are forced to snatch the wretched crumbs from each other's mouths'. Further, they are trapped in the ideology of the governing class which insists that 'revolt is the unnatural rather than the natural thing'. It is just this process, in all its complexities and confusions, that Shakespeare puts before us.

The text of the 1623 Folio confuses speakers in this scene, but those modern commentators who discern identifiable personalities emerging in the debate are surely right. Thus the Second Citizen is uneasy about proceeding against Caius Martius in view of the 'services he has done for his country' (25–30). But the First Citizen believes that Martius is motivated by pride rather than love of country. That he is speaking from knowledge rather than scoring a debating point is apparent from the alert way in which he adds Caius's further motive of pleasing his mother. But the Second Citizen's resistance to moving against an authority figure is dogged, however illogical: 'What he cannot help in his nature, you account a vice in him' (40–1). Unable to counter the First Citizen's accusations, he feebly insists that at least Martius is not covetous. Perhaps not, but he is soon confessing that he is drawn towards the sister sin of envy (229).

Meanwhile, progress towards the Capitol is stayed by the arrival of Menenius: 'one that hath always loved the people', says the Second Citizen. This sound unctuous, but even the First Citizen allows Menenius to be honest. It is really the mark of the latter's capacity to deceive. Later on, when he has a chance to assess the opposition at first hand, this Second Citizen – apt to think the best of people until faced with irrefutable evidence – grows firm in his opposition to Coriolanus (II.iii.83, 156–7, 160–2). So Shakespeare is emphasising, in this sudden turnabout, the remarkable fair-mindedness to be found among these citizens.

Menenius is the ideal spokesman for the governing class during this emergency. He is a shrewd operator, aware that people are flattered by the attentions of those they recognise as their social superiors. The iron fist is concealed by the velvet glove of an easy, familiar manner. But the message is clear about the futility of opposing the ship of state, divinely instituted and powered. At the helm are the patrician senators 'who care for you like fathers,/When you curse then as enemies' (76–7). While not swallowing that, the First Citizen is at least prepared to hear the belly-fable.

This resorts to the old notion of the body politic, the state as living organism. Its essential message is hierarchical. (That it is analogous to the contemporary view of the family with its patriarchal head is worth bearing in mind in connection with Caius Martius's family situation.) Menenius's picture of the body's members rebelling against the belly (the ruling class) provides an effective parable about the interdependence of the various elements in the state. The heckling and good-natured banter which accompany Menenius's fable shed light on his character as well as making the scene dramatically interesting. He is quick on his feet, able to keep up a genial front, and generally adept at cooling tempers. But there is more tact of manner than matter. He uses a belly-fable to listeners whose bellies are painfully empty. He pictures a system of food distribution from the centre when that is conspicuously lacking. In short, his friendly manner conceals a patronising contempt. He is the politican, well aware that in politics manner is more important than matter. Unhampered by any notions of social justice he can distract his stage audience from the real issues with a piece of pithy irrelevance.

Menenius's contempt appears naked when he declares that 'Rome and her rats are at the point of battle' (161). Rome is identified with the ruling class alone; the citizens are rats which plague the state. And he adopts another characteristic ploy in isolating the First Citizen as ringleader or 'great toe of this assembly' (154). Yet he offers a clear contrast with Caius Martius who now appears. At least Menenius tries to talk with the plebs. Martius flatly declares:

> He that will give good words to thee, will flatter
> Beneath abhorring. (166)

At this point, surely Menenius is the more dangerous to the plebeian cause. Martius is aloof, a clearly identifiable enemy. But Menenius is liked for his man to man affability. Where Martius is merely frightening, Menenius will flatter the plebs into self-betrayal.

To Martius the citizens seem equally detestable in peace and war: 'The one affrights you, /The other makes you proud' (168). His fierce indictment is the less persuasive since what he sees as an undifferentiated mass has been presented to us by Shakespeare as a collection of individuals. He is furious that they dare to

> cry against the noble Senate, who
> (Under the gods) keep you in awe, which else
> Would feed on one another. (185–7)

That any feeding on one another would have been precipitated by the Senate's failure to feed them is an unperceived irony. Indeed, Martius disdains to ask the citizens directly about their grievances. That he is fully aware of them becomes quickly apparent. But Menenius tells him anyway, in phrases clearly aimed at the plebs rather than Martius:

> [They want] corn at their own rates, whereof *they say*
> The city is well stor'd. (188–9)

He is giving nothing away and Martius fastens on to the same phrase:

> Hang 'em! They say!
> . . . They say there's grain enough? (189, 195)

He is outraged at their presumption, which he would repay with the sword:

> Would the nobility lay aside their ruth,
> And let me use my sword, I'd make a quarry
> With thousands of these quarter'd slaves, as high
> As I could pick my lance. (196–9)

The verb 'to pick', as used here, is virtually identical with 'to pitch'. The terms 'quarry' and 'quarter'd' work effectively because their primary application is to the hunting field rather than that of battle. Hence a 'quarry' is the pile of deer killed by hunters. To speak thus of the citizens associates with that animal name-calling in which Coriolanus and his fellows are wont to indulge at the expense of social inferiors.

But this is an odd performance. Coriolanus says himself that the citizens are no fighters, so why is he so eager to exercise his skills on them? This is a parody, even self-parody, of the vaunting super-hero. But as such it is a contribution to the play's critical consideration of the nature of heroism.

However, it now becomes clear why Coriolanus is so incensed against the citizens. When Menenius points out that his own artful words have sufficiently tamed this group of citizens, Martius announces that another group has won concessions to the extent of five Tribunes being appointed to represent the plebs in the Senate. This, he believes, is the thin end of a wedge directed against class privilege:

> The rabble should have first unroof'd the city
> Ere so prevail'd with me. (217–18)

News that war with the Volsces is imminent pleases Martius. He sees it as a means of killing off some of Rome's superfluous citizenry. So he recognises one half of a social contract: the duty which that citizenry has to fight for Rome. But he and his peers have no sense of reciprocal obligation. The senators have only yielded to pressure in giving the citizens some kind of representation.

Shakespeare has set up a sharp contrast between the citizens and Martius. Their estimate of him is accurate; his of them a tangle of ugly prejudices. If some of them are at fault in wishing to dispose of Martius, they at least have a specific target. He favours indiscriminate violence. He would rather see the very fabric of Rome destroyed than yield an inch to those he holds inferior (217–18). This is not merely a lack of political intelligence. The whole question of Martius's allegiance comes into view, casting a shadow forward to the events of Act IV, in his remarks on the Volscian leader Aufidius. He admires the latter immoderately as fighter, especially as opponent:

> Were half to half the world by th'ears, and he
> Upon my party, I'd revolt to make
> Only my wars with him. (232–4)

Already it is clear that Martius's military motives are personal, not patriotic.

The scene ends with the newly-appointed people's Tribunes, hitherto ignored, left on stage to assess Martius and his prospects in the war. They offer a shrewd analysis of the advantages likely to accrue to him as second-in-command, under Cominius, of the Roman force.

Act I, Scene ii

The scene shifts to a council of Volscian leaders. It indicates how the rival Roman and Volscian states continually spy on each other, something we recall when Coriolanus is accused of inconsistency for approving the use of deceit in war but not in peace (III.ii.41–5).

Ominously, intelligence from Rome claims that there is less hatred between Aufidius and Martius than between the latter and Rome. But Aufidius, forced on the defensive by the news of Rome in arms, resolves to settle personal as well as national scores.

Act I, Scene iii

This scene presents the wife and mother of Martius at their embroidery. We have already had a hint from the First Citizen of the mother, Volumnia's influence on her son. A primary motive behind the inclusion of this wholly Shakespearean scene is to explore the nature of this influence. What we learn is that Martius's chief defect, his limited humanity, is firmly rooted in this family environment. There is grotesqueness in Volumnia's daintily feminine activity while she discourses easily of slaughter. Her pride in Martius's warlike spirit shows that they are temperamentally very close. For her, killing is a manly quality (18), whereas even a reference to blood is disturbing to his wife, Virgilia (38). Virgilia is anxious about Martius's safety. Volumnia is concerned only with his acquitting himself honourably. The delusions of honour are a favourite Shakespearean preoccupation. They had been exposed by Falstaff, and again in *Troilus and Cressida*. Like her son, Volumnia is blinded by honour to the inhumanities of war and class hatred. She imagines him plucking 'Aufidius down by the hair' or urging on his citizen-army in authentic terms:

> 'Come on you cowards, you were got in fear
> Though you were born in Rome.' (30–4)

A note of perversity is immediately apparent in Volumnia's words: 'If my son were my husband I should freelier rejoice in that absence wherein he won honour, than in the embracements of his bed, where he would show most love' (2–5). The urgencies of sexuality are translated to the field of military endeavour, a tendency of thought found elsewhere in the play. But, beyond that, there are intimations of more than maternal feeling in Volumnia's choice of image.

Another aspect of the sexual process is given a disquieting turn as she rebukes Virgilia for squeamishness:

> The breasts of Hecuba
> When she did suckle Hector, look'd not lovelier
> Than Hector's forehead when it spit forth blood
> At Grecian sword contemning. (40–3)

These twin aspects of Hector, as baby and as corpse, work rather like one of those Renaissance paintings where the Christ-child lies on his mother's lap in a pose which prefigures her supporting of the crucified Christ. But the latter is a fruitful coalescence, a reminder of man's being born again, not born merely to be butchered on the battlefield. Volumnia is fascinated by death, not resurrection. For her, the fantasy bravado of Hector's spitting blood at the very sword which has killed him is high fulfilment.

Volumnia shows a tendency for this discordant telescoping of ideas. Warrior and harvester come together with unexpected results:

> His bloody brow
> With his mail'd hand then wiping, forth he goes
> Like to a harvest man that's task'd to mow
> Or all, or lose his hire. (34–7)

The notion is common enough, relying on the symbolism of Death the harvester. But what these lines emphasise is not a symbolic figure of rhythmic, purposeful destruction. They embody the harsh realities of agricultural life where the labourer must submit to overwork or starve. Unconsciously, Volumnia is establishing a bond between her son and the despised peasant.

The arrival of a family friend serves several purposes. Enquiry about Martius's child reveals him to be a chip of the old block; excited by marching men and deriving satisfaction from tearing a pretty butterfly to pieces (55, 65). But it also shows that Martius's wife, although softer-tempered than the family into which she has married, nevertheless has strength of character. She refuses to allow either friend or mother-in-law to talk her out of her determination not to leave the house until Martius returns from the fighting. What Volumnia represents is the classic idea of Roman virtue. The very word derives from *vir* (man), pointing to the supremacy of the virtues of manliness, bravery and military prowess. But these would not be the priorities of Shakespeare's world, where a different lifestyle required a different scale of moral values. What Shakespeare shows through Virgilia is that espousal of a more humane set of values may denote strength rather than weakness.

So Virgilia is not lacking in moral strength, though her quiet manner might seem underpowered as an influence on her husband compared with Volumnia's fierce eloquence. Coriolanus himself, in the tender moment of his homecoming, addresses her as his gracious silence (II.i.174). It is the moment which moves Wilson Knight to claim that 'her silent tears . . . speak more than many volumes' (*The

Imperial Theme, p. 174). But precisely because she is so quiet, where Volumnia – like her son – is full of sound and fury, any competition between these two for the soul of this man must be unequal. And it is the soul of a man that is at stake in the play.

However, this scene offers more than an insight into Coriolanus's psychological shaping. It illuminates links between personal background and the larger social issues of the play. Virgilia's humanity only emphasises the general shortage of that commodity in Coriolanus's world.

Act I, Scene iv

News of Martius's besieging Corioli, delivered at the end of the previous scene, sets the stage for this one. The Coriolan senators address the invading Romans from the parapet of their town hall (i.e. the gallery in Shakespeare's theatre). Ladders are called for to enable the besiegers to scale the wall. But the Volsces anticipate the danger and rush out to engage the Romans. Martius welcomes battle as his proper element. But his troops are forced back and he curses them foully:

> All the contagion of the south light on you,
> You shames of Rome! You herd of – boils and plagues
> Plaster you o'er, that you may be abhorr'd
> Farther than seen, (30–3)

He is so angry that he becomes inarticulate. To him these men have the souls of geese; they have 'run/ From slaves that apes would beat' (35–6). He feels keenly the ignominy of his own part in the retreat. They must turn again and re-engage.

> Or, by the fires of heaven, I'll leave the foe
> And make my wars on you. (39–40)

Fear is a favourite inducement to combat. But the user would be well advised to lead from behind. As Martius impetuously pursues the withdrawing Volsces through their own gates, he finds himself alone. He is thought dead, but hacks his way clear. The Romans under Lartius seize the chance to storm the gates and enter Corioli.

Act I, Scene v

The town is being sacked. It is easy for Martius, a man of substance, to show contempt for paltry plunder. The spoils of war were apt to be the only payment seen by the common soldier. But Martius is right to give priority to assisting Cominius, who confronts the main enemy force. Martius's eagerness to relieve Cominius, however, may have less to do with loyalty than with his obsession to continue a personal feud with Aufidius. He makes light of his wounds and leaves Lartius behind to hold the town while he goes to seek more glory.

Act I, Scene vi

In Scene viii Martius, no doubt for tactical reasons, disclaims serious wounds. But he is obviously a terrible sight, resembling someone who has been flayed (22). He is none the less welcome to Cominius, who has been hard pressed by Aufidius. They embrace and Martius is oddly reminded of when he wooed and bedded his bride:

> Oh! let me clip ye
> In arms as sound as when I wooed; in heart
> As merry as when our nuptial day was done,
> And taper burn'd to bedward. (29–32)

The excitement of battle is still upon him. We have noticed the way that Volumnia sensualises killing in Scene iii. The perversity of confusing bridal couch and battlefield is here underscored by Martius's ghastly appearance. Like the Bloody Sergeant in *Macbeth* he personifies the horrors of war.

Asked how Lartius is coping, left to occupy the captured town, Martius describes how he is busy

> Condemning some to death, and some to exile,
> Ransoming him, or pitying, threat'ning th' other;
> Holding Corioles in the name of Rome,
> Even like a fawning greyhound in the leash,
> To let him slip at will. (35–9)

Here, observes Jan Kott perceptively, 'war is suddenly objectified' in what is a 'universal representation of any occupation . . . It questions the whole system of values defended by Martius' (*Shakespeare Our Contemporary*, p. 155). Kott also points to the devastating irony of making Martius himself the unknowing critical spokesman

But Martius is keen for more action, cutting short Cominius's enquiry about his own doings in terms hardly suited to a subordinate:

> Where is the enemy? Are you lords o' th' field?
> If not, why cease you till you are so? (47–8)

He asks to be placed opposite the enemy's crack troops, led by
Aufidius, and calls for volunteers to go with him. He would have only
such as

> think brave death outweighs bad life,
> And that his country's dearer than himself. (71–2)

But he has caught the mood of the moment and is overwhelmed by
the response. The troops bear him off shoulder high.

Act I, Scene vii

Switching locations for a brief scene is a feature of *Antony and
Cleopatra*, written about the same time as *Coriolanus*. It is a clear
indication of the flexibility of the Globe stage. This scene shows
Lartius anxious to join his fellow generals against Aufidius. He
sensibly judges that a small garrison will serve to hold the town for a
brief period. If the Romans lose the main battle, the town will
become untenable anyway.

Act I, Scene viii

This is another brief scene on paper, but on stage it would have lasted
for some time. Martius and Aufidius are the two great rivals, allowing
a set-piece fight of a kind much appreciated in the early theatre. The
sword was still a key weapon, and there would be many in the
audience able to appreciate the finer points.

To render the fight inconclusive Shakespeare resorts to a favourite
device of the time: Aufidius receives unwelcome assistance, leaving
him master of the field but somewhat crestfallen:

> Officious, and not valiant, you have sham'd me
> In your condemn'd seconds. (14–15)

Something of the flavour of a formal duel is caught here. Active
participation by seconds in a duel seems to have been acceptable
practice in France, but certainly not amongst Shakespeare's country-
men.

Act I, Scene ix

Ultimate victory lies with Rome, and Cominius testifies to Martius's
enormous contribution. He vividly anticipates the effect his news will

have when they return to Rome. Timid ladies will let their fascination get the better of their fear, and even the hostile citizens will be obliged to 'thank the gods/Our Rome hath such a soldier' (5–9). Lartius, too, joins in praising Martius. For him Martius 'is the steed, we the caparison' (12), the great war horse to whom the rest are only trimmings. We have to see this in relation to their wager in Scene iv, where the importance of the good horse is apparent, and Lartius is able to anticipate his present graceful compliment to Martius (iv, 6–7). Whereas Cominius's offer to Martius of a tenth of the captured horses and treasure is disdainfully refused (31–8), the gift of the commander's own horse has special meaning amongst these warriors and can be accepted (59–61).

Either payment or praise would, for Martius, somehow profane the sacred act of killing. It is profanation when the martial trumpets are sounded in his honour. The forms of battle must stay clean and hard, untouched by the sycophancy of courts. He says something of the sort in a textually corrupt speech (41–6). But an earlier speech gives us our best opportunity of evaluating his distaste for praise:

> Pray now, no more. My mother,
> Who has a charter to extol her blood,
> When she does praise me, grieves me. I have done
> As you have done, that's what I can: induc'd
> As you have been, that's for my country.
> He that has but effected his good will
> Hath overta'en mine act. (13–19)

Even his mother, who has special privileges, disturbs him with her commendations. He resents his comrades' marvelling over his latest exploits. If they gave him his due, expected the highest professional performance from him as a matter of course, there would be no occasion to marvel. He commands respect but has no need for praise. Like the brilliant centre-threequarter, he has scored a hat-trick of tries but wants no more than a nod of appreciation from the team captain.

If there is vanity here, it is subordinated to more important considerations. What confronts us is the real key to Martius's character. He is a soldier above all, a true professional. That is why later on he can shift allegiance to the Volscian side. It is less a shift than a reaffirmation of his true allegiance to the craft of soldiering. He may talk here, in all honesty, of his duty to Rome; but that duty only compels while it is consonant with his higher duty to the military ethic.

If he is gratified to be known as Coriolanus, victor of Corioli, that is because it is a suitably abstract tribute. But both this and the tumultuous acclaim following Cominius's announcement are splendidly undercut by his 'I will go wash' (66). He cuts an attractive enough figure at this stage. He has but one request, that a kindly man with whom he lodged in Corioli should be given his freedom. Martius had seen him captive, but his humanitarian intentions had been deflected by the appearance of his arch-rival Aufidius. Now it is battle again, or at any rate the exhaustion resulting from his efforts in the field, which defeats his warmer impulses. He cannot remember the man's name to secure his release.

This is really the tragedy of Martius, or Coriolanus, as he must henceforth be called: that his integrity as a person is dominated by his integrity as a soldier. But that is not to say that we should drop our reserve towards someone whose values have been shaped, however honestly, by his commitment to man-killing.

Act I, Scene x

This scene shows how matters look to the defeated general. He refuses to see himself as part of the Volscian defeat. Yet he, too, is a defeated man – defeated five times by Coriolanus. This sours him. Henceforth, since fair means are of no use, he will resort to whatever is needed to bring his enemy down. This is the soldier become politician when direct methods prove ineffectual. It is a shift which Coriolanus is not only utterly unwilling to make on principle, but one of which he is temperamentally incapable. Coriolanus's future banishment is prefigured in Aufidius's voluntary exile as he withdraws to lick his spiritual wounds. But that he has only withdrawn temporarily from the game is indicated by his instruction for intelligence to be brought to him in his place of retreat.

ACT II

Summary
All Rome eagerly awaits news from the front. Success for Martius, or Coriolanus, will mean the opportunity for political power. But his contempt for the plebs attracts the hostility of the new people's Tribunes. They intrigue against him, but his outstanding achievements in the field make him a popular choice for consulship. Although unwilling to canvas the people's support, he is prevailed upon to do so. But his grudging attitude makes the Tribunes persist in their opposition.

Act II, Scene i

The scene is Rome, where news of the battle is anxiously awaited. For Menenius and his party the situation is straightforward. They propose using Coriolanus's expected success to have him elected consul. For that very reason, the Tribunes have mixed feelings about a Roman victory. They see Coriolanus as a beast of prey. Menenius unpersuasively reverses the metaphor to suggest that Coriolanus is a lamb assailed by a wolfish populace. Brutus scoffs: 'He's a lamb indeed, that baes like a bear' (10). A dispute over Coriolanus's alleged pride brings out some of the real issues:

MENENIUS: You blame Martius for being proud.
BRUTUS: We do it not alone, sir.
MENENIUS: I know you can do very little alone, for your helps are
            many, or else your actions would grow wondrous single.
            (31–6)

Menenius betrays the perennial fear of the socially elite: that the underprivileged will band together and use their collective power to reorder society. This is what underlies his unremitting flow of insults and mockery. He professes to be more of a convivial person than man of affairs: 'one that converses more with the buttock of the night than with the forehead of the morning' (50–2). When people represent themselves, as he does here (52–3), as plain, outspoken fellows, it is as well to look out for trickery. His preference may well be for nights of love and liquor, but it takes political chicanery to ensure their continuance.

We now experience one of those frequent moments in the play where the patricians' rudeness to the plebs is conspicuously set against the courtesies which they exchange amongst themselves. Manifestly, Menenius finds Volumnia and her party more congenial company than the plebs. These new arrivals bring news of Coriolanus's return, and Menenius asks whether he is wounded less out of sympathy than because wounds have political currency. Talk of wounds distresses Virgilia, while for Volumnia they are the red badge of courage (117–22). But Volumnia, too, recognises the value of fresh scars in Coriolanus's bid for a consulship (146–8). Yet whereas Menenius savours electioneering rhetoric – 'every gash was an enemy's grave' (154) – Volumnia is more perceptive about what war entails. Of Coriolanus she remarks that 'before him he carries noise, and behind him he leaves tears' (157–8). She may be little moved by suffering, but she understands its place in her son's activities.

Coriolanus looks in the same direction for words to brush away his wife's tears:

> Ah, my dear,
> Such eyes the widows in Corioles wear,
> And mothers that lack sons. (176–8)

Tender concern is wedded to a strange insensitivity. The bereaved women of Corioli weep, but not those of Rome. Bereavement only tears at the entrails of the defeated foreigner. The Roman women who have suffered loss are, by implication, sustained by the fact of being on the winning side, but still more by the military ethic which deems it a triumph to fall on the field of honour.

The Tribunes have been silent witnesses to this scene. They recognise that people of every condition will be talking of nothing but Coriolanus or struggling for some vantage point, even the rooftops, from which to see him. But they are also very clear about the consquences for themselves of his being made consul (220–1). He has no time for plebeian representation. But it is precisely his 'soaring insolence' from which they take comfort (222–4, 252). He will not dissimulate humility in the customary vote-seeking fashion. His intemperate nature will betray him in the political arena, and they must aid the process (243–51). Their analysis of the situation and what they must do is accurate and entirely in accord with the interests of their class. But for the moment the progress of this war hero is unstoppable, when even the nobles genuflect as if ' to Jove's statue' (264). Perhaps we should pause over this phrase, since it was written at a time when physical images, as an aid to worship, were widely frowned upon in Britain. Elsewhere Coriolanus is likened to a god, but here only to an image of divinity. None the less, this is an event of such euphoria and magnificence as cannot be encompassed on stage. Instead it is evoked in the report of a messenger, who comes to summon the Tribunes to the Capitol.

Act II, Scene ii

Two officers enter to prepare the Capitol for the arrival of the senators. But their real purpose is to present, in dramatic terms, some of the issues underlying the forthcoming election. Coriolanus is the clear favourite: 'That's a brave fellow', declares the First Officer, 'but he's vengeance proud, and loves not the common people' (5–6). But is his contempt as bad, wonders the Second Officer, as the flattery which brings so many to power? Besides, the people are fickle, and 'for Coriolanus neither to care whether they love or hate him manifests the true knowledge he has in their disposition' (12–14). But the First Officer argues that Coriolanus is not merely indifferent about how they feel towards him; he actively courts their hatred. Is that not as bad, he asks, as to court their favour with flattery? But still the Second Officer resists bracketing him with 'supple' flatterers: 'He hath deserved worthily of his country' (24). There is no time for further argument, and the First Officer cuts it short by professing agreement (35).

Patricians and Tribunes assemble and the two sides of the issue are explored more elaborately. For Cominius and his party, the main business is to eulogise Coriolanus for his conduct in the war. The Tribunes are differently inclined and Brutus artfully seeks to needle Coriolanus into indiscretion. But it is less this activity than the formal praise which discomforts Coriolanus, forcing him to quit the chamber. Menenius turns venomously on the Tribunes:

> Masters of the people,
> Your multiplying spawn how can he flatter . . . ? (77–8)

They represent the proletariat, mere child-breeders. This class is necessary to the economy, or in time of war as what would later come to be known as cannon-fodder. But it is otherwise worthless. Its reputation for vigorous breeding is itself a source of apprehension. This is the fear which puts edge on Menenius's phrase about 'multiplying spawn'. Already in the last scene (34–6) we have heard Menenius voicing the familiar apprehensions of the small power-group about the sheer numbers over which it exercises tenuous control. Now those apprehensions are focused in this envenomed figure of subhuman fecundity.

From this, Shakespeare switches us abruptly, and purposefully, to Cominius's encomium on Coriolanus's military career. After one kind of terror we are confronted with another. From an alleged subhumanity we turn to an alleged superhumanity which is still more appalling.

The speech is considered in detail below (Section 6). It is sufficient to note here how it forms a prelude to Coriolanus's appearance before the Senate and his expressed unwillingness to follow the custom of canvassing the people's support:

> I cannot
> Put on the gown, stand naked, and entreat them
> For my wounds' sake to give their suffrage. (136–8)

Menenius recognises the trap which is opening up; but the Tribunes, intent on closing it, properly insist that the constitutional process be observed (139–41).

Act II, Scene iii

Here Coriolanus stands before the people in customary fashion to win their vote. Shakespeare achieves a remarkable breadth of sympathy in this scene. He makes us feel for Coriolanus who endures paroxysms of embarrassment. That Coriolanus is no respecter of custom was apparent in the previous scene. Now he tries to associate it with error. Custom threatens the purity of Coriolanus's reactionary vision; submit to it and

> The dust on antique time would lie unswept
> And mountainous error be too highly heap'd
> For truth to o'erpeer. (118–20)

But he does submit up to a point, getting through the miserable business by undercutting it with fierce mockery.

The citizens' uncertainty is similarly painful. They recognise that their involvement in the process is limited. Thus, if Coriolanus carries through his side of the affair, they are morally obliged to do likewise: 'We have power in ourselves to [withhold our vote], but it is a power that we have no power to do' (4–5). They allow his unusual honesty, but cannot mistake his total contempt for themselves. The Third Citizen sums up: 'if he would incline to the people, there was never a worthier man' (39–40).

But even as they choose him, they know they will never gain his goodwill. The Tribunes ask them why, in that case, they gave him their support (172–4). But the question is rhetorical since these worldy-wise Tribunes know that it is often the way of the voter to make a rod for his own back.

It is the Tribunes who now receive the angle of sympathy, having coached the plebs in election technique to no avail. The voters were to have pressed Coriolanus for an election promise which he might have granted, though he was more likely to have lost his temper. Whereupon

> You should have ta'en th' advantage of his choler,
> And pass'd him unelected. (196–7)

But all is not yet lost. The election result has still to be ratified. And the prevention of this becomes the new goal of the Tribunes. Lay the blame on us, they suggest, for persuading you to vote for Coriolanus against your better judgement. Astutely, they plan to arrive at the Capitol before the crowd:

> And this shall seem, as partly 'tis, their own,
> Which we have goaded onward. (260—1)

Their methods are a little devious, then; they are politicians making a bid for power. But there is some justice in their view of themselves as channels through which the public will may be released.

ACT III

Summary
Coriolanus goes to meet the people, but the Tribunes warn that they are in ugly mood. Coriolanus is impatient and speaks out in terms which are construed as treason by the Tribunes. They fail to arrest him but he must answer their charges. Volumnia recommends tact and he agrees to play the politican. But the Tribunes goad him into revealing his true feelings and he is banished from Rome.

Act III, Scene i

The scene opens with a discussion of the Volscian situation. Although Aufidius has re-armed, there is doubt about whether this represents an immediate threat to Rome. Coriolanus asks, with heavy anticipatory irony,

> At Antium lives he? . . .
> I wish I had a cause to seek him there. (17–19)

But attention swings quickly to domestic affairs. The Tribunes attempt to dissuade Coriolanus from entering the market-place, where the people are roused against him. Despite Menenius's cautions, he is incensed against those who seek 'To curb the will of the nobility' (38). Not to respond decisively would mean yielding to 'such as cannot rule/Nor ever will be rul'd' (39–40). Notions of breeding, of being born to rule, surface continually. Sicinius cleverly links two sets of ideas:

> If you will pass
> To where you are bound, you must inquire your way,
> Which you are out of, with a gentler spirit,
> Or never be so noble as a consul. (52–5)

Coriolanus's physical progress towards the market-place super-imposes on that towards a consulship. He is taking a wrong route, unmindful that it is gentleness of spirit rather than of birth which must confer the nobility of office.

Coriolanus is provoked. But it is also a matter of principle with him to declare fiercely against the people. Not to do so is to nourish the 'cockle of rebellion' (69). So, while he allows himself to be baited by the Tribunes, the matter runs far deeper. That those Tribunes should have been appointed at all represents the beginnings of a nightmare reversal of social order. It is not his way to mince matters, and he tells his peers that 'You are plebeians/If they be senators' (100–1). He favours a hardline policy. The establishment of the Tribunes was a concession wrung from the patricians during a riot. It is an aberration to be corrected. To make concessions of any kind to the lower orders must be construed as a sign of weakness which, like Athenian experiments in democracy, will feed 'The ruin of the state' (116–36).

To the Tribunes this represents treason, and they would arrest Coriolanus, calling on the people for aid. For once Menenius is too demoralised to speak. Blunderingly he looks to Sicinius to ease matters; but Sicinius is no patricians' lackey:

SICINIUS [to the people]:   You are at point to lose your liberties:
                          Martius would have all from you, Martius
                          Whom late you have nam'd for consul.
MENENIUS: This is the way to kindle, not to quench.
FIRST SENATOR: To unbuild the city and to lay all flat.
SICINIUS: What is the city but the people? (192–7)

There are two Romes, one of the rich and one of the poor. Menenius's fable of the belly has no bearing on the realities. This is not an organically unified state, but one divided by class interests. Coriolanus would preserve that division absolutely, so the Tribunes urge his death. Menenius at last finds his voice, and attempts to repair the damage. But he knows it is too late once Coriolanus draws his sword. Only violence will serve now.

But even against larger numbers, the well-armed, well-trained patricians have the advantage. They drive off the people, though larger crowds are expected imminently. Coriolanus is only persuaded to leave with the utmost reluctance. But his politically wiser friends perceive that there is more than an immediate danger in risking a situation where the citizens will learn to 'overbear/What they are us'd to bear' (247–8).

Menenius is left behind to provide a choric summing up of events. He agrees that Coriolanus 'has marr'd his fortune':

> His nature is too noble for the world:
> He would not flatter Neptune for his trident,
> Or Jove for's power to thunder. His heart's his mouth:
> What his breast forges, that his tongue must vent;
> And being angry, does forget that ever
> He heard the name of death. (253–8)

The speech is full of irony from the first line, its foreshadowing of later, tragic events colouring our response. The concept of nobility has already come under Sicinius's probing scrutiny (54–5). Now Menenius, the nobleman, finds nobility an irritant in an ignoble world. So, too, while *flattery* supplies moral weight to the next line, that its potential objects are divinities, not mere mortals, hints that the nobility may be commixed with arrogance. Ironic possibilities continue to mount up. 'His heart's his mouth' might suggest an engaging forthrightness. But it is rooted in Ecclesiasticus, 'The heart of fools is in their mouth', so is undercut with a biblical pronouncement on folly.

But these reflections are interrupted by the clamour of the returning crowd, led by the Tribunes:

SICINIUS: Where is this viper
> That would depopulate the city and
> Be every man himself? (261–3)

Sicinius's opening words have to be apprehended in the context created by those of Coriolanus, who easily and persistently sees the people in terms of a many-headed hydra, a 'bosom multiplied', or 'multitudinous tongue' (92, 130, 155). He is the Herculean hero whose role it is to smite off the monster's heads. To Sicinius this is properly not just an inhuman viewpoint but a traitorous one, one which demands the death penalty. But Menenius has recovered his persuasive powers, arguing that Coriolanus is not a disease requiring the sharpest surgery:

> he's a limb that has but a disease:
> Mortal, to cut it off; to cure it, easy. (293–4)

He then invokes Coriolanus's war record, to which Sicinius responds shortly, 'This is clean kam' – so much eye-wash (302).

But the Tribunes are eventually persuaded to more constitutional means against Coriolanus. They are at heart reasonable people who recognise the difficulty of decrying Coriolanus's violent solutions while espousing similar solutions themselves. In the light of subsequent events, of course, this raises an awkward question about the preference for reason over violence. In terms of sheer political expediency the Tribunes are wrong not to become killers like Coriolanus. They have seen the dilemma clearly:

> To eject him hence
> Were but our danger, and to keep him here
> Our certain death. (284–6)

As usual, Shakespeare provides no pat answer to an acute moral problem, but forces it uncompromisingly on our attention.

Act III, Scene ii

This scene finds Coriolanus, presumably at home, expressing himself with the extravagance of a hero of the pre-Shakespearean theatre:

> Let them pull all about mine ears, present me
> Death on the wheel, or at wild horses' heels,
> Or pile ten hills on the Tarpeian rock,
> That the precipitation might down stretch
> Below the beam of sight: yet will I still
> Be thus to them. (1–6)

He is quite innocent of political guile, and wonders why his mother is not more wholly approving since she it is who evidently nurtured his contempt for the plebs. He is obsessed with being true to his nature (15), but she cynically recognises the relationship between power and the assertion of identity:

> I would have had you put your power well on
> Before you had worn it out . . .
>   lesser had been
> The thwartings of your dispositions, if
> You had not show'd them how ye were dispos'd,
> Ere they lack'd power to cross you. (17–23)

Since Coriolanus admits the place of dissembling in war, argues Volumnia, why should he deny it in peacetime (46–51)? Even now, she says, Coriolanus can impose upon the plebs. In this Menenius concurs, testifying to that generosity which he correctly, if sardonically, associates with their folly:

> This but done,
> Even as she speaks, why, their hearts were yours:
> For they have pardons, being ask'd, as free
> As words to little purpose. (86–9)

But going into the market-place is a prospect which fills Coriolanus with real horror:

> To th' market-place!
> You have put me now to such a part which never
> I shall discharge to th' life. (104–6)

He would be acting a part – the theatrical image doubles the sense of deception – quite foreign to his nature and capabilities. He would be walking into a totally alien and distressing scene. He apprehends the market-place in the terms found in *Troilus and Cressida*, where everything is dirty, sordid and full of 'Good traders in the flesh'. Ironically, even the noble trade of arms in that play is reduced to the same squalid, knowing terms:

> ULYSSES: 'tis meet, Achilles meet not Hector:
> Let us (like merchants) show our foulest wares
> And think perchance they'll sell.

The message of *Troilus and Cressida* is that war, like prostitution, is a trading in human flesh. But just as Coriolanus could never accept that viewpoint, so is he quite oblivious to the communal meaning of the market-place uppermost here.

Philip Brockbank, in the Introduction to his edition of *Coriolanus* (p. 17), indicates 'Shakespeare's concern to establish the market-place as an element in the city's political topography (e.g. II.ii.159, III.ii.131)' But the political and social enmesh in this locale. For the citizens, as we see very clearly at the start of IV.vi, the market-place is not only a place for trade. It is a place for social intercourse, encompassing human relations moral as well as material. It has emblematic force as a meeting-place where the main activities are of a morally informed kind, not simply dedicated to the profit motive.

Again we must invoke the Act IV speech of Sicinius's (vi. 8–9) in support. But a place where the several classes of society could intermingle, as in the Elizabethan theatre, must seem hateful to Coriolanus. That he would be going there in a manner to trade himself off to social inferiors only adds the final degrading touch. But at the combined insistence of Menenius and his mother, he teeters on the brink of acquiescence:

> Well, I must do't
> Away my disposition, and possess me
> Some harlot's spirit! (110–12)

The sense of prostituting himself is strong. His 'throat of war' will be reduced to a eunuch's (113–14). It is loss of dignity which he cannot face. The thought of it saps his resolution. His mother's powers of persuasion are exhausted:

> To beg of thee it is my more dishonour
> Than thou of them. (124–5)

She chides him for his pride and, in spite of all, her outburst is successful. This is a foretaste of her far greater exertions in V.iii, a first proof of her power over him so decisive that we have no difficulty in accepting the second. Under its influence he must go against the grain of his character and resolve again to play the politician:

> I'll mountebank their loves,
> Cog their hearts from them, and come home belov'd
> Of all the trades in Rome. (132–4)

Warned that the Tribunes will be ready with their accusations, he replies:

> Let them accuse me by invention: I
> Will answer in mine honour. (143–4)

But Menenius, knowing the danger of that honour, cautions: 'Ay, but mildly'.

Act III, Scene iii

The patricians must pursue a policy of concealment and deception. Meanwhile, the Tribunes plan how best to penetrate that front:

> BRUTUS: In this point charge him home, that he affects
> Tyrannical power. If he evade us there,
> Enforce him with his envy to the people. (1–3)

Their power derives from the numerical strength of the people. This is less cohesive, so much more tricky to manage, than the patricians' source of power. They seek to arrange that whatever sentence they pronounce on Coriolanus shall be reinforced by the collective voice of the people. But, as before, their immediate ploy must be to arouse Coriolanus's anger so that 'he speaks/What's in his heart' (28–9).

It is sometimes argued that Shakespeare balances the two sides perfectly, and it is certainly true that the Tribunes are as intent on gaining a measure of power as the patricians are on retaining it. Yet we are obliged to notice that while the people are intent on trapping Coriolanus into telling the truth, his friends require him to lie. It is the way that Coriolanus is caught between friends and enemies that, despite his unattractive qualities, compels our sympathy. Now, before his examination by the Tribunes, Menenius must intrude, cautioning the people not to be offended by Coriolanus's soldierly manner, and getting further mileage out of his military record:

> The warlike service he has done, consider: think
> Upon the wounds his body bears, which show
> Like graves i' th' holy churchyard. (49–51)

Coriolanus's embarrassment is clear in his dismissive 'Scratches with briers,/Scars to move laughter only' (51–2). The rhetorical cunning which Menenius showed during that first scene of riots has deserted him. His attempts to manipulate Coriolanus have proved too much, and his judgement is gone. Even Cominius tells the old man to shut up (57). After these preliminaries, Sicinius has no difficulty in riling Coriolanus. The charge that he is 'traitor to the people' (66) sets him off, and he is hardly placated by Brutus's intervention to the effect that 'he hath/Serv'd well for Rome' (83–4). John Palmer (*Political Characters in Shakespeare*, p. 292) offers this as an example of the Tribunes' fair-mindedness. But Coriolanus's explosive response to what he considers the effrontery of comparing

Brutus's civic service to that of the battlefield has surely been counted on:

CORIOLANUS: What do you prate of service?
BRUTUS: I talk of that, that know it.
CORIOLANUS: You? (83–5)

Nor need any particular apology be made for Brutus's tactics here. He is the political street-fighter who can make headway only by attending more to ends than means. At least, unlike Aufidius, the Tribunes never stoop to making false accusations against Coriolanus. It is hard to believe that the latter's popularity amongst the Volscians is due to anything as uncharacteristic of him as flattery (V.vi.23–4).

Now sentence of banishment is pronounced, and it is Cominius's turn to speak of service to the state, by virtue of which he claims the right to intervene:

> I do love
> My country's good with a respect more tender,
> More holy and profound, than mine own life,
> My dear wife's estimate, her womb's increase
> And treasure of my loins. (111–15)

There is dignity and power in Cominius's words. When he declares that his ties to Rome are stronger than those of family, we recognise a genuine expression of values flirted with earlier in Menenius's belly-fable. He begins to develop a conception of how the individual should dedicate his virtue and creativity to the political and moral advancement of the state.

The Tribunes cut Cominius short, not because they suspect his sincerity but because what he says is utterly beside the point on which they are intent. As John Palmer remarks in a slightly different context, 'Tribunes of the people have notoriously little respect for professions of altruism and of stainless regard for the public welfare uttered by their social superiors' (p. 260). This must be especially so when these social superiors operate from a premise which would exclude the Tribunes and those they represent from any considerable role in the perceived political structure. Although Cominius may be more high-minded than Menenius, he espouses the same brand of reactionary politics.

For his political opponents, Cominius's words have been only a respectable front for the kind of sentiments to which Coriolanus now gives incautious expression. The latter's words may be sharpened by present anger and embitterment. But his basic attitude towards the citizens has remained unchanged throughout. Here these images of putrefaction reflect damagingly on the speaker; they are a mark of his own sickness:

> You common cry of curs! whose breath I hate
> As reek o' th' rotten fens, whose loves I prize
> As the dead carcasses of unburied men
> That do corrupt my air. (120–3)

The assertiveness of '*my* air' is capped by the superb arrogance with which he reverses the process of banishment: 'I banish you!' (123). This is more than mere rhetoric. There is a sense in which he considers himself to be the essential Rome. He has yet to develop and refine this idea, and the process will be purely destructive. Indeed, Sicinius's words to the effect that Coriolanus 'would depopulate the city and/Be every man himself' (III.i.262–3) are curiously pertinent here. There are already intimations of this final solution as he enjoins the citizens to

> here remain with your uncertainty!
> Let every feeble rumour shake your hearts!
> Your enemies, with nodding of their plumes,
> Fan you into despair! (124–7)

Uncertainty is the most terrible affliction of cowards, such as he conceives them to be. But his assessment of them is by no means precise. They will remain undisturbed by feeble rumours, and enjoy a hitherto unparalleled period of contentment in his absence. The plumes destined eventually to fan them into despair will be his own. He leaves himself out of the calculation in judging them their own worst enemies. Nor will they continue to exercise their new-won power of banishment to their own detriment until, shorn of all protectors, they are finally delivered.

> as most
> Abated captives to some nation
> That won you without blows. (131–3)

He has never seen them aright, so is hardly likely to give them their due under present circumstances. Even so, an intangible threat hangs heavy in the air as he is driven to the gates by a jeering throng. It has been observed that this moment, as the gates close upon him, 'reverses his initial triumph, when the gates of Corioles shut him in alone of all the attacking Romans' (Levin, *Shakespeare and the Revolution of the Times*, p. 196). The 'ironic pattern' will be completed when the citizens of Corioli finally turn on him and precipitate his death.

ACT IV

Summary
Coriolanus is expelled from Rome and joins up with Aufidius who is preparing to march on Rome. Meanwhile, the Roman citizens enjoy a period of peace and prosperity until news arrives of the approaching danger. Aufidius, envious of Coriolanus's popularity amongst the Volsces, plans to turn on him after Rome has fallen.

Act IV, Scene i

Coriolanus takes his leave of family and friends at the gates of Rome. He is impatient of the women's tears and resorts to his usual style of disparagement of the people: 'The beast/With many heads butts me away' (1–2). He points out how 'common chances common men could bear' (5), but he

> Will or exceed the common, or be caught
> With cautelous baits and practice. (32–3)

But ironically this will prove a false antithesis. While he may 'exceed the common', this will not save him from those 'cautelous baits'.

The extent of his friends' loyalty is apparent in Cominius's readiness to accompany him for a month (38). On the other hand, Coriolanus's loyalty consists in being true to himself. It is in this way that personal integrity and his betrayal of Rome may be reconciled. There is anticipatory irony but no deception when he declares on parting:

> While I remain above the ground you shall
> Hear from me still, and never of me aught
> But what is like me formerly. (51–3)

Act IV, Scene ii

The Tribunes are now concerned to disperse the excited crowd. Their political wit, a desire to build bridges rather than burn them, is set in deliberate contrast to Coriolanus's mode of proceeding:

> Now we have shown our power,
> Let us seem humbler after it is done
> Than when it was a-doing. (2–5)

Menenius, Virgilia and Volumnia approach, and the Tribunes are anxious to avoid the latter. She is in turbulent humour after bidding farewell to Coriolanus, and begins spitting venom immediately. Virgilia remains virtually silent and is rebuked by Volumnia for her 'faint puling' (52). Menenius's role, too, is subordinate, as would-be peacemaker. He shows himself in accord with Volumnia's sentiments – 'You have told them home' (48) – but not with her blunt methods. He recognises the lasting harm resulting from confrontation politics.

Sicinius responds to Volumnia's imperious anger with 'Are you mankind?' (16). It is tantamount to asking if she is crazy. Violent anger is deemed the prerogative of the male. In a woman it is to become perverse, virago-like. Volumnia chooses to misunderstand, taking him to mean 'Are you human?'; she responds by attributing a bestial ingratitude to Sicinius:

> Hadst thou foxship
> To banish him that struck more blows for Rome
> Than thou hadst spoken words? (18–20)

It is a curious commentary on Coriolanus that even his staunchest advocate, his mother, can never get beyond his killing prowess in praising him. His very blows are 'noble', balanced against Sicinius's 'wise words' (21). The intention is to deny wisdom to Sicinius. But the effect is to elevate violence over reason. For her, language must be as violent as Coriolanus's activities in the field:

> I would my son
> Were in Arabia, and thy tribe before him,
> His good sword in his hand . . .
> He'd make an end of thy posterity,
> Bastards and all. (23–7)

It is her way to 'lament . . . /In anger, Juno-like' (52–3). The allusion is to the judgement of Paris, the Trojan prince, which went against Juno in favour of Venus. In requital, Juno brought about the destruction of Troy. Hence there is irony here, it being Volumnia's lot to save a city rather than to destroy it. But that time is not yet. For the moment, violence of language serves vicariously for violent acts. The acts are still to be preferred. Later, Volumnia herself will initiate a new phase in which, as Harry Levin puts it (p. 190), 'speech-making triumphs ironically over war-mongering'.

Act IV, Scene iii

The scene is set a day's journey from Rome (12). It prepares the ground for Coriolanus's joining with Aufidius. Nicanor, a Roman traitor, meets a Volscian who has been sent to locate him. They talk of the rioting in Rome, about which the Volscian is already well informed. But he is surprised to learn of Coriolanus's banishment. The consequent unrest will make a splendid opportunity for the Volscian invasion of Rome which has been in active preparation: 'I have heard it said, the fittest time to corrupt a man's wife is when she's fallen out with her husband' (31–3).

Act IV, Scene iv

Coriolanus enters wearing '*mean apparel*'; he has come to the '*gown of humility*' in very truth. In the process he acquires fresh complexity. It is a growth which transforms the warlord into tragic hero. The process is not unfamiliar in Shakespeare. *Richard II* offers something comparable as the spotlight shifts from political issues to human drama in the later stages of the play.

This new complexity finds expression in Coriolanus's only soliloquy. He appears strangely vulnerable as he arrives disguised in a Volscian town. Here in Antium, amongst his long-standing enemies, he can even venture a touch of humility as he never would in more congenial surroundings. His immediate reflection is 'Tis I that made thy widows' (2), so the very women and children have ample cause to turn on him:

> know me not;
> Lest that thy wives with spits, and boys with stones,
> In puny battle slay me. (4–6)

There is wry acknowledgement here that, whereas on the battlefield Coriolanus has wrought havoc amongst the husbands and fathers, when he is weaponless his savage skills are worth little. In sufficient numbers – he has made many widows and orphans – and armed with nothing but their anger and kitchen utensils, even weak women and children would outmatch him.

Indeed, so it comes to pass. Coriolanus is not a man to be defeated on the battlefield. He will fall victim to the toils of family, which he has so often ripped apart. It will be women and a child who eventually work his downfall, though they will be Roman and not Volscian.

But for the moment he seeks directions to the house of Aufidius, pausing on the way to soliloquise on mutability:

> O world thy slippery turns! Friends now fast sworn,
> Whose double bosoms seems to wear one heart,
> Whose hours, whose bed, whose meal and exercise
> Are still together, who twin, as 'twere, in love
> Unseparable, shall within this hour,
> On a dissension of a doit, break out
> To bitterest enmity: so fellest foes,
> Whose passions and whose plots have broke their sleep
> To take the one the other, by some chance
> Some trick not worth an egg, shall grow dear friends
> And interjoin their issues. (12–22)

In seeing the world thus in a state of flux, he can represent his proposed defection to the enemy as part of the normal, natural process. In his favour it should be noted that his situation differs decisively from that of Nicanor. Rome has cast him out, made him a stateless person, so he must look for acceptance elsewhere. He has no idea what reception he will get from Aufidius, but must take his chances. Since he no longer owes allegiance to a state which has disowned him, he will respond in kind to favourable treatment.

Yet there is more than pragmatism at work here. When Coriolanus took his leave of friends and relatives at the city gates, we might reasonably have assumed that his ties to one Rome at least, that of the patricians, would remain intact. But now we recognise an implacable hatred directed even at a Rome thus narrowly conceived: 'My birthplace hate I' (23). The factional issue which formerly loomed so large with him, has yielded to a total emotional rejection already intimated in his snarling response to the order of banishment: 'I banish *you*!' (III.iii.123).

Act IV, Scene v

This is the key scene in which Coriolanus and Aufidius meet for the first time without drawn swords. Coriolanus's attempts to enter Aufidius's house, where a party is in progress, are thwarted by servants due to his unprepossessing appearance. But his looks are more than uncouth. His exchange with the Third Servant suggests something deeply sinister. If his blood-soaked appearance in I.vi had concealed his identity, making him seem the god of battles, he now has the look of Death. But there is something of Death the jester here, full of bitter ironies and dark absurdities. In answer to the servant's question, he claims to dwell 'Under the canopy' in 'the city of kites and crows', the carrion-feeders (39, 43). Aufidius remarks on his 'grim appearance' and quite fails to recognise him (61). He asks, over and over, 'thy name? . . . Speak man: what's thy name?' (54–5). As Philip Brockbank puts it in his Arden edition of the play (p. 252), 'The repetition of *name* reaches an almost incantatory intensity'. After the sixth appeal, Coriolanus discloses his identity, adding that his surname is Coriolanus (69). It is a name for which he had a bloody baptism, a name connoting death.

He quibbles on '*sur*name'and the '*serv*ice' for which it was given (69, 71). It ironically links with the service which he has declared himself ready to offer at the end of the preceding scene, service now to the erstwhile enemy. It is the very last word of Scene iv, and it is picked up in the first line of the next when it is trivialised as the service provided at table. The two kinds of service, of domestic attendant and of warrior, become confused with sexual service during the exchange with the Third Servant:

CORIOLANUS: I serve not thy master.
THIRD SERVANT: How, sir! Do you meddle with my master?
CORIOLANUS: Ay; 'tis an honester service than to meddle with thy
                 mistress. (46–9)

There is an echo of that image of adultery used by Nicanor to point up Rome's vulnerability (IV.iii.31–3). In the process it raises the teasing question of whether the service which Coriolanus is about to offer is more honest than that of the adulterer.

Coriolanus's lengthy speech to Aufidius is profoundly revealing in this respect. Having disclosed that he is Coriolanus, he complains that the name is all the reward he ever got from his 'thankless country' (71). Loot never appealed to him; but this suggests that mere abstractions were insufficient, too. What remains is senatorial office, with its power and authority, implicitly seen here as a proper return for enduring the hazards of war.

We now fully understand how Coriolanus's extreme bitterness at having been thwarted in his bid for office has spilt over into hatred of his fellow patricians. It is these 'dastard nobles' who conferred on the plebs the power to banish him (76). They, too, are culpable, so his proposed vengeance will encompass them. If Aufidius will join him, he will fight

> Against my canker'd country with the spleen
> Of all the under Fiends. (92–3)

Aufidius responds by embracing Coriolanus ecstatically. Like Coriolanus when he hugged Cominius on the battlefield (I.vi.29–32), Aufidius thinks back excitedly to his wedding night:

> more dances my rapt heart
> Than when I first my wedded mistress saw
> Bestride my threshold. (117–19)

These bridal occasions have sometimes been perceived as a refined and delicate form of combat. Conversely the emotions of battle are somewhat akin to the sexual impulse. Aufidius confesses to something like an infatuation with Coriolanus; each night he has

> Dreamt of encounters twixt thyself and me –
> We have been down together in my sleep,
> Unbuckling helms, fisting each other's throat –
> And wak'd half dead with nothing. (124–7)

The affinity with erotic dreams needs no emphasis. Now the prospect of this union in battle produces a heated intensity in which sexual and military cravings and urgencies coalesce. Their joint energies will be released in the rape of Rome; the sexual violence is clear in that image of 'pouring war/Into the bowels of ungrateful Rome' (130–1).

These two leave the stage to the servingmen, the mood dropping from high drama into comedy. But in addition there is commentary on what has taken place, and a parodic restatement of the protagonists' military ethic. The servants marvel at the power which is exuded by Coriolanus, or crudely demonstrated by his strength of arm. They warily consider him the fighting superior of their own master (150–75).

The Third Servingman enters with the news that Coriolanus is being feted, given a seat of honour at the head of Aufidius's table: 'Our general himself makes a mistress of him, sanctifies himself with's hand, and turns up the white o' th' eye to his discourse' (199–202). The play of hands and the attentiveness to Coriolanus's every word are the tokens of the lover. The picture is a vivid replay of what we have already seen enacted between the protagonists. Those intimations of cruelty which the psychologist detects beneath the toyings of courtship will achieve an awesome reality when this couple moves on Rome. War, says the Second Servingman, pursuing the image, is 'a ravisher'. Yet the naked display of force is given moral ascendancy over its opposite, for 'it cannot be denied but peace is a great maker of cuckolds' (234–5).

The moral contrast is pursued as the First Servingman offers the paradox that peace 'makes men hate one another'. It is expressed as an amusing conundrum, solved without difficulty by the Third Serving-man: 'because they then less need one another' (236–8). Yet the humour disguises a real moral dilemma, one often considered in relation to the Second World War blitz. The solidarity which that outside threat achieved amongst the British people could never be recaptured in the years of peace which followed.

The case for war is put very plainly. When it arrives, says the Second Servingman,

> We shall have a stirring world again, This peace is nothing but to rust iron, increase tailors, and breed ballad-makers.
> FIRST SERVINGMAN: Let me have war, say I. It exceeds peace as far as day does night; it's sprightly walking, audible, and full of vent. Peace is a very apoplexy, lethargy; mulled, deaf, sleepy, insensible; a getter of more bastard children than war's a destroyer of men. (225–32)

War for Coriolanus is more than a bracing activity. The conflict with the Volsces had seemed a way of disposing of the plebeian threat. Now war is to be the surgery practised directly on his 'canker'd country' (92). So far from being a necessary evil, a regrettable means to a desirable end, war is seen as a source of moral and spiritual renewal. Its destructive aspect is nothing compared with the corrupting ease of peacetime. Indeed, the destructive aspect is part of war's appeal. In *Antony and Cleopatra*, written about the same time as *Coriolanus*, Shakespeare describes death's coming in terms of 'a lover's pinch/Which hurts and is desir'd'. Here the same powerful fascination is ascribed to war. That it is a perverse fascination, that the dynamic creativity of its chief exponent is in truth a destructive futility, is underlined by putting this martial philosophy into the mouths of several comic servingmen. That they have been sharp enough to see the absurdity of Aufidius's feting of Coriolanus makes no difference to the fact that we must look twice at the wisdom of jesters.

Act IV, Scene vi

The scene is a bustling Roman street, as Sicinius intimates in his reference to 'Our tradesmen singing in their shops' (8). He claims that the patricians would take no pleasure in the new atmosphere of peace, since it results from the Tribunes' decisive action in banishing Coriolanus. Certainly the Tribunes deserve some credit for the improved morale of the citizenry, and indeed Menenius acknowledges that things are going well under their direction (16). If Sicinius's tone when remarking that Menenius 'is grown most kind/Of late' (11–12) is a touch sarcastic, at least the social rifts are temporarily papered over. Following a rehearsal of Coriolanus's faults, it is only the idea that he had been intent on a throne which Menenius attempts to controvert. But news that the Volsces are on the march against Rome restores the initiative to Menenius. The Tribunes know their political careers are on the line should it prove true. So they are desperate to have it found idle rumour, especially when the still more demoralising report arrives that Coriolanus has joined forces with the Volsces.

Even Menenius finds this hard to believe, but it is confirmed by Cominius. His vehement forecast of what must follow recalls his extraordinary eulogy of Coriolanus before the Senate (II.ii.103–22). The Volsces bring rape, pillage, total destruction. Coriolanus

> is their god. He leads them like a thing
> Made by some other deity than nature,
> That shapes man better; and they follow him
> Against us brats, with no less confidence
> Than boys pursuing summer butterflies,
> Or butchers killing flies. (91–6)

We recall Coriolanus's son 'mammocking' a butterfly (I.iii.65). Cominius's speech sets the tone of awe in which Coriolanus's martial reputation is held by the Romans. But when he adds 'He'll shake your Rome about your ears' (100), a new note is heard. The dissociation between upper and lower classes is complete. It is exactly as the Tribunes say (6,151–2): this patrician is perversely willing to suffer himself in order to have the satisfaction of seeing the plebs damaged.

The beginning of the scene shows the citizens at their best, but now they are at their worst – frightened, fickle, and contradictory:

> though we willingly consented to his banishment, yet
> it was against our will. (145–6)

In this atmosphere it would be easy to take Brutus's mention of his 'wealth' (160) as an intimation that he has been using his office to his financial advantage. But this should be resisted just as the idea that Coriolanus is ambitious to become king should be resisted. Brutus is a substantial citizen, keenly aware of what he has to lose.

Act IV, Scene vii

The scene shifts to the Volscian forces. Aufidius discusses with his lieutenant Coriolanus's amazing popularity amongst their troops. It is as if the soldiers are bewitched by him (2), and we recall the way that Coriolanus has inspired the Roman troops in times past (I.vi.76). But Coriolanus has been continuously successful in this way since joining the Volsces, a conspicuous contrast with his total failure to charm the Roman citizenry.

Aufidius is irked to be in Coriolanus's shadow, but must put the present cause before personal feeling (6–8). Opportunity will present itself later on for dealing Coriolanus's pride a blow. Meanwhile, he should be the means of taking Rome without a struggle, as the fish was supposed to yield itself up to the osprey (34–5). Aufidius's thoughts grow disjointed from this point. He speculates on the cause of Coriolanus's downfall in Rome. But, whatever the cause, 'he has a merit/To choke it in the utt'rance' (48–9). The thought is not easy to follow. Perhaps the merit to which Aufidius refers is Coriolanus's proven capacity as soldier to mesmerise the Romans into submission. But

> our virtues
> Lie in th' interpretation of the time. (49–50)

Aufidius understands that circumstances determine whether or not what we do, or are, is found praiseworthy. What was a fault in Rome when Coriolanus was banished will now appear a virtue. Later, when the time is ripe for Aufidius to assert himself, it will again become a fault by means of which Coriolanus may be destroyed.

Aufidius is quite perceptive here about those character traits which might be construed faults in Coriolanus. Not only pride but deficiency of judgement is noted, as well as that rigidity which has inhibited his moving 'From th' casque to th' cushion' – from the theatre of war to that of politics (43). Any one of these could get sufficiently out of hand to work his downfall. But when Aufidius attributes open boasting to Coriolanus, the accusation seems unwarranted (a pre-echo of those other apparently groundless charges in V.vi.23–6). In these last lines of this extraordinary speech, as Aufidius's excitement mounts at the prospect of getting the better of his old rival, his thoughts crush together in a species of verbal indigestion.

ACT V

Summary
Pressed by the Tribunes, a reluctant Menenius attempts to dissuade Coriolanus from sacking Rome. He is disappointed, and it is left to Volumnia to prevail upon her son. But her success proves fatal for Coriolanus. He has now become vulnerable, and Aufidius seizes the chance to have him assassinated.

Act V, Scene i

The great issue to be settled in this last act is whether Coriolanus will persist in taking his revenge on the city of his birth or whether pride and resentment will yield to stronger, perhaps finer, feelings. In the latter event, an important secondary consideration would be whether such yielding is a sign of strength or weakness – or even both at once.

The act begins strongly with Menenius refusing to go and appeal to Coriolanus. 'Go you that banish'd him', he advises sardonically:

> A mile before his tent fall down, and knee
> The way into his mercy. (4–6)

Cominius has already made overtures to Coriolanus as a former comrade-in-arms, but without success:

> 'Coriolanus'
> He would not answer to; forbad all names;
> He was a kind of nothing, titleless,
> Till he had forg'd himself a name o' the' fire
> Of burning Rome. (11–15)

Clearly it would be indiscreet to maintain the name 'Coriolanus'. But in abandoning all names Coriolanus is rejecting his past – home, family and friends. Indeed, he has to all intents shed his former identity. At several points Cominius has described him as a 'thing' (II.ii.109; IV.vi.91), a fighting automaton. But to be 'nothing' is to have severed all those ties which shape one's identity. He will forge himself a new identity, 'Romanus', in the ashes of Rome.

As for friends and relatives,

> He could not stay to pick them in a pile
> Of noisome musty chaff. (25–6)

It is an extension of thoughts expressed in Act I: war is a useful way of ridding Rome of unwanted plebs, that 'musty superfluity' (I.i.16; 225). There is a fine consistency here. Coriolanus has never considered the citizens as part of the real Rome. He is Rome, and in the destruction of the city may truly bear the name 'Romanus'.

The anger and anguish of Menenius are translated into venom which he spits at the people: 'We must be burnt for you' (32). The sharp division of national interests is clearly apparent here. It is comparable with that Second World War exhortation.

> YOUR courage,
> YOUR cheerfulness,
> YOUR resolution,
> Will bring US Victory!

– issued before it was remembered that in wartime it is needful to pretend that there is but one nation. As Sicinius says, and there is dignity in his reply,

> If you refuse your aid
> In this so never-needed help, yet do not
> Upbraid's with our distress. (33–5)

But there is more than ordinary fear underlying Menenius's refusal to plead with Coriolanus. He is afraid of the personal hurt – he would be 'grief-shot with his unkindness' (44–5) – should Coriolanus reject him. Yet eventually he persuades himself that when Cominius was rejected Coriolanus must have been out of sorts, or perhaps had not eaten. After

> wine and feeding, we have suppler souls
> Than in our priest-like fasts. (55–6)

But Cominius knows there is no hope unless Coriolanus's wife and mother can be persuaded to intercede.

Act V, Scene ii

Menenius has arrived at the Volscian camp. The guards refuse to admit him, even when he urges that Coriolanus is his greatest friend. In former times, he assures them, he has sung Coriolanus's praises even to excess, prompting the bawdy quibble that he shall not pass even 'though it were as virtuous to lie as to live chastely' (26–7). Beyond that, falsehood becomes associated with Rome, truth with the Volsces:

SECOND WATCH: Howsoever you have been his liar, as you say you
have, I am one that, telling true under him, must
say you cannot pass. (30–2)

But irony is a governing principle of this play. When the First Watch declares that Coriolanus's anger is not to be dispelled by 'the easy groans of old women' or 'the virginal palms of your daughters' (41–2), there is anticipation of the embassy of women in the next scene.

Coriolanus and Aufidius enter, just as the watchmen threaten to drive Menenius away by force. Now it is Menenius's turn to threaten as he puffs himself out in the pride of his special relationship with Coriolanus. He calls Coriolanus 'son' (69–70), and we are reminded forcibly of Henry V's rejection of Falstaff in *Henry IV, Part II*. Falstaff, too, had been apt to see himself as a father to the younger man. Whereas affairs of state distracted Henry's father from his parental function, there is perhaps in Menenius's expressions of fatherly feeling an oblique reminder that Coriolanus had no real father on hand during his formative years.

Coriolanus makes his rejection of Menenius a proof of his fidelity to the Volscian cause. He leaves Menenius to the mockery of the watchmen, though the old man's show of spirit in a painful situation impresses the First Watch. But the Second, exemplifying that hero-worship which has been said to be rife amongst the Volsces, is more affected by Coriolanus's display: 'he's the rock, the oak not to be wind-shaken' (108–9).

Act V, Scene iii

In this next scene, however, the oak is to be moved by the wind of his mother's entreaty. And there is further irony in the way that Coriolanus prides himself on stony denial of Roman appeals just before Volumnia's arrival:

>   This last old man,
> Whom with a crack'd heart I have sent to Rome,
> Lov'd me above the measure of a father,
> Nay, godded me indeed. (8–11)

He has been esteemed a god, but appears all too human as his resolve to see no more Romans weakens instantly on the arrival of his mother, wife, child and Valeria. Or perhaps such yielding brings him closer to the gods (see V.iv.24); though there is more apt irony in the fact that he is yielding to the very one who has done most to shape that in his character which has produced the present dilemma. It is a dilemma finely rendered in the line

>   Let it be virtuous to be obstinate. (26)

The violence of Coriolanus's fight to preserve such obstinacy is witness to the strength of his normal feeling for family. Still toying with the notion of divinity, Shakespeare has him attribute to his wife's doves' eyes' power to 'make the gods forsworn' (27–8). All too conscious of his mother's power over him, he seeks to act as if he were 'author of himself' (36). But the futility of such an attempt is already clear in the telling circumlocution – 'the honour'd mould/ Wherein this trunk was fram'd' (22–3) – by which he has just described his mother.

 Still determined to take his revenge, he has become uncertain in the role 'Like a dull actor' (40). He kisses his wife, and can only think of how he has remained faithful to her (48). He kneels before his mother to show his 'deep duty', quibbling on the marks which his knees make in the ground (51). Volumnia suggests ironically that it is her duty to kneel to him, but he sees in this a monstrous inversion of nature. If this were to be suffered, then any kind of outrageous possibility might be made a trivial occurrence:

> What's this?
> Your knees to me? to your corrected son?
> Then let the pebbles on the hungry beach
> Fillip the stars. Then let the mutinous winds
> Strike the proud cedars 'gainst the fiery sun,
> Murd'ring impossibility, to make
> What cannot be, slight work! (56–62)

To describe the winds as 'mutinous' is to bring the turmoil which he contemplates in inanimate nature squarely into the human context. A failure of simple duty to a parent effectively symbolises Coriolanus's revolt against Rome. That he fails to perceive the ramifications of his own words is hardly important. This expression of traditionalist sentiment is hugely encouraging to Volumnia, who responds in terms calculated to weigh with Coriolanus:

> Thou art my warrior:
> I holp to frame thee. (62–3)

She introduces Valeria, who is known to Coriolanus as

> The moon of Rome, chaste as the icicle
> That's curdied by the frost from purest snow
> And hangs on Dian's temple! (65–7)

This is a different Valeria from the fun-loving young woman of I.iii. But she is better suited to the occasion, the coldness of her chastity not only according with Coriolanus's own but also poised against the heat of threatened violence.

Volumnia continues to play her cards in immaculate succession, next presenting Coriolanus's son, 'a poor epitome' who must be allowed time to grow and develop (68–70). But Coriolanus still holds his position:

> Do not bid me
> Dismiss my soldiers, or capitulate
> Again with Rome's mechanics. (81–3)

It is not so much loyalty to the Volsces' cause as to his soldiers which concerns Coriolanus; while the favourable impression wrought by his family is negated by renewed thoughts of the hated plebs. He insists that his mother make her plea publicly before the Volsces (92–3); and she shows how she, too, is faced with a dilemma of divided loyalties:

> either thou
> Must as a foreign recreant be led
> With manacles through our streets, or else
> Triumphantly tread on thy country's ruin,
> And bear the palm for having bravely shed
> Thy wife's and children's blood. (113–18)

She has been forced to choose country rather than her son, but she recognises that a straight appeal of that kind will achieve nothing with him. Coriolanus may be induced to respond to the demands of family, but he has never been given to thinking in terms of larger loyalties. So she emphasises what the destruction of Rome would mean in more narrowly conceived but highly potent terms. Thus, if her words fail to stop Coriolanus, then he must trample on his mother's womb in his march on Rome. Virgilia echoes the sentiment:

> Ay, and mine,
> That brought you forth this boy to keep your name
> Living to time (125–7)

The procreative aspect of their case is powerfully emotive. The self-destructive dimension, if young Martius is to fall victim to his father's vengeance, has a special resonance in view of Coriolanus's disowning of his name.

Coriolanus attempts to leave them, but his mother detains him with a long and crucial speech. She is not only bent on bringing Coriolanus to a fundamental shift of attitude but shows that she has already undergone one herself. How much has it cost her to declare that 'Thou know'st, great son,/The end of war's uncertain' (140–1), or to turn his having 'affected the fine strains of honour' (149) against him? With such strength at her command, she needs no direct assistance from her companions: her appeal to the tearful Virgilia to speak – 'He cares not for your weeping' (156) – is surely rhetorical. But she uses their presence effectively. There is complex irony in her claim that 'There's no man in the world/More bound to's mother' (158–9). Coriolanus makes another attempt to leave and she falls on her knees, a pose which must deeply offend his filial sensibility. Now she senses she has won, confidently asking to be dismissed; and concludes with the splendidly evocative lines

> I am husht until our city be afire,
> And then I'll speak a little. (181–2)

The understatement of that short line, coming at the end of this great impassioned speech, has a fine potency.

Coriolanus is silent, holding his mother by the hand, before giving expression to his emotional prostration:

> Behold, the heavens do ope,
> The gods look down, and this unnatural scene
> They laugh at. O my mother, mother! O! (183–5)

The metrical irregularity of that last line reflects his inner turmoil. It gains a cosmic dimension from the picture of the gods looking down as on a theatrical scene. The scene is 'unnatural' partly because his mother still kneels to her son, but still more so because he, against his nature, has yielded.

Coriolanus may have pawned something of his honour as a soldier at this point, but it is here that he acquires full tragic stature. Too often in the past he has been blind to the implications of his actions. Yet this time he is well aware of the extreme, perhaps fatal, hazard which he runs. 'But let it come', he adds (189), in what the Arden editor describes as 'a tellingly simple tragic formulation'.

But he is by no means defeatist. He now turns his attention to Aufidius, assuring him that 'though I cannot make true wars, /I'll frame convenient peace' (190–1). He would like to hear Aufidius admit that in like circumstances he would have acted similarly. But the latter answers shortly, 'I was mov'd withal' (194). Privately, however, Aufidius resolves to use Coriolanus's change of heart to his own advantage.

Act V, Scene iv

Meanwhile, in the city Menenius assures Sicinius that the women's embassy will have been in vain:

MENENIUS: See you yond coign o' th' Capitol, yond cornerstone?
SICINIUS: Why, what of that?
MENENIUS: If it be possible for you to displace it with your little finger, there is some hope the ladies of Rome, especially his mother, may prevail with him. (1–6)

This imagery of the city and its buildings is rife throughout the play. It imparts a solidarity to the urban scene, even while its inflections are often towards the imminent destruction of Rome, its walls and institutions. What gives Menenius's words a special impact is the fact that we have knowledge which he lacks. We know that Coriolanus has already capitulated. Are we to glean, then, that in this capitulation the Tribunes will have come to some heightened power on the Roman scene?

What follows, in which two salient aspects of Coriolanus's character are placed side by side, is also heavily qualified by the scene just witnessed between Coriolanus and his mother. The two aspects we are shown are that of Coriolanus as destructive force, and as one that 'loved his mother dearly' (15). The former is represented in Menenius's notion of his developing 'from man to dragon' (13). There is no criticism intended, but we recall those Act IV associations of Coriolanus with a dragon (i.30; vii.23). Curiously enough, the more benign aspect comes in as an interjection from Sicinius, who speaks with the optimism of desperation. Menenius refuses to take comfort, partly because of his own recent experience with Coriolanus and partly because he relishes the discomfiture of the Tribune.

With our additional knowledge, we recognise a sense in which Coriolanus, the martial automaton, is no more than a memory. But it is a memory which is being enforced here through a repetition of key terms. 'When he walks, he moves like an engine' (18–19) echoes Cominius's speech before the Senate (II.ii.107–8). He is godlike, the culmination of a whole string of references (III.i.80; IV.vi.91; V.iii.28, 150); and when he is described as 'a thing made for Alexander' (22) we register not only that he is an image of the great Greek conqueror but that several times he has been described as a *thing*, dehumanised (II.ii.109; IV.v.117; IV.vi.91).

Menenius's voice of doom is dramatically reinforced by the arrival of a messenger. He reports that Brutus is being manhandled by the crowd, which threatens to kill him unless the embassy of women is successful. But a second messenger follows to announce that it *has* been successful, an event as momentous as the expulsion of the Roman kings (44).

Act V, Scene v

This brief scene shows the reception given to the women when they return from Coriolanus's camp to Rome. It is an opportunity for pageantry, and functions ironically both as parallel to Coriolanus's own triumphant return to Rome in Act II and as contrast to the scene which follows where he meets his ignominous fate. The latter irony is especially sharp in view of the fact that the patricians have not neglected to make political capital out of Volumnia's success.

Act V, Scene vi

Aufidius plots against Coriolanus out of envy. Now that Coriolanus has provided him with the pretext, he seeks to undermine his popularity, for it has rankled to seem 'his follower, not partner' (39). Aufidius makes his bid through the nobles, for the common people still hero-worship Coriolanus. (Their attitude has been strangely at variance with that of their Roman counterparts in this respect.) There is some ambiguity about whether the action is set in Aufidius's home town, Antium (50) or Corioles, scene of Coriolanus's greatest triumph. Aufidius marvels that the people, 'Whose children he has slain', should cheer Coriolanus so heartily (53).

When Coriolanus enters with his troops, his speech proclaims the military advantages and financial profits he has gained for the Volsces' slurring over the attendant betrayal:

> Hail Lords, I am return'd your soldier,
> No more infected with my country's love
> Than when I parted hence, but still subsisting
> Under your great command. You are to know
> That prosperously I have attempted, and
> With bloody passage led your wars even to
> The gates of Rome. Our spoils we have brought home
> Doth more than counterpoise a full third part
> The charges of the action. We have made peace
> With no less honour to the Antiates
> Than shame to th' Romans; and we here deliver,
> Subscrib'd by th' consuls and patricians,
> Together with the seal o' th' senate, what
> We have compounded on. (71–84)

Stanley Hussey makes a sharp point about this speech. These generalities and subordinate clauses contrast with Coriolanus's previous modes of utterance: 'He has finally learned to talk like a politician, to present a defeat as a victory, but in so doing he debases himself. For all his previous inflexibility, we admired him more when he spoke like a Roman' (*The Literary Language of Shakespeare*, London, 1982, p. 174). The very language he uses exposes the ambiguity of his action in yielding to his mother. Humanity and hypocrisy have somehow become entwined.

But this is just for our ears. Aufidius registers none of this complexity, only the chance to destroy his rival. He refuses to address him by his 'stol'n name/Coriolanus, in Corioles' (89–90), calling him traitor instead. It is a tactic which the Tribunes have already put to effective use, and Aufidius follows up by taunting him as 'boy of tears' (101). The sting in this, as Harry Levin points out, stems from the fact that, in heeding his mother's persuasions, 'the strong man becomes again – as it were – a child' (*Shakespeare and the Revolution of the Times*, p. 195). But there is immaturity in Coriolanus's predictable loss of control, too. He threatens to beat Aufidius, but then, with a monstrous lack of tact, recalls how

> like an eagle in a dove-cote, I
> Flutter'd your Volscians in Corioles. (114–15)

In thus reminding the people of the painful bereavements which he has caused them, he is doomed. The conspirators stab him to death and Aufidius tramples the corpse, moving even the Volscian nobles to protest:

> Thou hast done a deed whereat valour will weep. (132)

For all the harm Coriolanus has done them in the past, and their present sense of betrayal, they recognise his exceptional qualities:

> Let him be regarded
> As the most noble corse that ever herald
> Did follow to his urn. (142–4)

Or, more cynically, perhaps they reflect that heroes may be praised safely when dead. Perhaps there is a mixture of cynicism and something more. Aufidius, too, changes his tune:

> My rage is gone,
> And I am struck with sorrow. (146–7)

He helps to bear off the body that he has abused moments before, vowing that Coriolanus 'shall have a noble memory', a monument commensurate with his stature (153). But what is this nobility, which can accommodate the betrayal of both homeland and that of adoption? Nor does the confusion end there since paradoxically, and in spite of himself, this double apostate has contrived to die for his country. Aufidius's words form a fittingly enigmatic conclusion, since he is hardly to be reckoned an impartial judge of greatness or nobility.

Wilson Knight's succinct evaluation of Coriolanus has him 'In war a man of death, in peace . . . a social poison'. Yet finally he is 'purified' through an act of love (*The Imperial Theme*, Methuen, 1965, pp. 181, 197). But if Aufidius discerns nobility in his enemy, it is not in this newly revealed capacity for love but in his uniquely destructive capability. The play ends with a dead march, like *Hamlet*. But unlike *Hamlet*, indeed uniquely in mature Shakespearean tragedy, it offers no signs of renewal, no Fortinbras to take up the reins and restore order out of chaos. Instead, with or without Coriolanus, this world remains stubbornly out of joint.

4 THEMES AND ISSUES

4.1 SHAKESPEARE AND HISTORY

Clearly, as a dramatist Shakespeare enjoys a latitude unavailable to the historian. But, equally clearly, he was fascinated by the historical process and the historian's task. History plays were in vogue before Shakespeare: dramatists could gain authority for their works by basing them on historical writings. But it was Shakespeare who brought the ambitious sweep of the history cycle on to the English stage.

He began in conventional fashion, by drawing moral lessons from past lives and events. But the *Henry IV* plays cut deeper, just as the late Roman plays do. Now his concern is with meaning, with probing those factors which go to shape our lives and actions.

This growth of sophistication is apparent in Renaissance historiography, too. Although much historical writing still followed the old patterns of the Wheel of Fortune – the idea of the swift rise to greatness followed by an equally precipitous fall – it was increasingly acknowledged that the configurations of history were seldom so conveniently regular. By overtly straining the figure Holinshed's *Chronicles of England, Scotland, and Ireland*, which stands in the same relation to Shakespeare's English history plays as Plutarch's *Lives* stands to the Roman plays, draws attention to the figure's limitations.

Thus while Coriolanus's career may seem to follow this broad pattern, we should avoid the glib attractions of such an explanation as much as those of the tragic flaw. To talk of the *flawed* hero is redundant, since his shared humanity ensures that he is flawed. It is one of the ironies of dramatic criticism that the latter notion – bequeathed to us by Aristotle, that least dogmatic of great thinkers – should have become such an article of faith.

4.2 THE CLASSICAL WORLD

Although concern with the ancients was no new thing, with Shakespeare's contemporaries it had reached obsessional proportions. Engagement with the literary culture of ancient Greece and Rome, especially the latter, was thought to endow man with the dignity of the philosopher; and the dignity of man is something which was very powerfully urged during the sixteenth century. Nevertheless, reverence for the ancients provoked a measure of iconoclasm, and Shakespeare takes deft advantage of this. Hence, when Valeria mocks Virgilia as 'another Penelope' (I.iii.82), we remember that the latter was a favourite emblem of chastity, whose assiduous tapestry-weaving kept her suitors at bay during her husband's absence at the Trojan war. So, by encouraging Virgilia to leave her embroidery, Valeria is virtually inviting her out on the town.

Not only the literature of ancient Rome but its history and institutions were studied as object lessons. Shakespeare's turning to Coriolanus stands, according to Terence Spencer ('Shakespeare and the Elizabethan Romans', *Shakespeare Survey*, 10, 1957, p. 35), as one of the great feats of the historical imagination in Renaissance Europe. Spencer takes this view in the knowledge that the Elizabethans would have found the Rome of the Caesars more congenial. *Julius Caesar* and *Antony and Cleopatra* both deal with the period of the break-up of the Republic. But in *Coriolanus* Shakespeare chooses to present a phase soon after the dispossession of the kings and the birth of the Republic. The pattern of government at that time, with no single authority-figure, would have seemed outlandish in Shakespeare's day, when Europe offered nothing remotely parallel. Even the Venetian Republic had its doge. Indeed, since Plutarch is so vague about constitutional details, Shakespeare has drawn a far more democratic picture than in fact existed by showing the plebs involved in Senate elections.

Variant patterns of government were under heavy scrutiny in Shakespeare's day. Venice, or Poland with its elective form of monarchy, offered much food for thought. So did the British institutions from earlier times. In the first years of the century, the Society of Antiquaries seems to have grown increasingly preoccupied with political and constitutional questions – a potentially dangerous activity, which may help to explain its dissolution in 1607. A founder-member, Robert Cotton, had established a collection of books and manuscripts which he hoped would form the basis of a national library. But the threat of such an archive to the ruling elite was readily perceived, and the King closed the library in 1629. So it was the more accessible testimony from ancient Rome – an essential feature of every grammar-school curriculum – to which educated people had regular recourse.

4.3 POLITICS

Politics is an important link between that intense cultural involvement with the ancient world and the immediacies of Jacobean England. Indeed, the Roman setting might offer some cover to a dramatist intent on dealing with hard political issues. But the cover would be pretty threadbare since classical precedent was regularly invoked during the incessant disputes of King James's first Parliament (1604–10). While it has been suggested that in representing a nearly headless state Shakespeare was avoiding suspicion that his real concern was the Jacobean regime, it could equally be urged that the question of absolutism, embodied in the character of Coriolanus, is a prime Jacobean issue. If political schism was still a long way off, James lacked Elizabeth's adroitness. She demonstrated the technique of divide and rule over a long reign of forty-five years. James, who came to the throne on her death in 1603, managed to unite a large section of the House of Commons into articulate opposition.

This is a situation fairly reflected in *Coriolanus*, a play which goes far beyond the other Roman plays in its concern with class conflict. Coriolanus is hardly a James I. His approach has a brutal directness about it altogether alien to James. But he does manage, even more decisively than James, to polarise friends and opponents into irreconcilable groups destined to tear the state apart. The conflict itself is posed not in Jacobean terms but in the ancient opposition of Nature and the Law. Coriolanus stands for Nature. This means belief in himself and his own strength without regard for others. To demand complete freedom in the way that he does is necessarily to infringe the freedoms of others. Freedom and tyranny are ever apt to be obverse and reverse of the same coin. He is the strong, determined, clear-sighted superman, with the capacity and self-confidence to escape from conventional restraints.

These restraints (the Law) are the attempts of the weak to protect themselves from natural man, so they have no binding power on him. But what the Tribunes set out to show is that there is a strength in unity which goes beyond that of any one man, or small elite, however remarkable. So, as the ancient philosophers had shown, the terms become confused. If the greatest strength came to lie with the convention-governed masses, would they not thereby have Nature as well as Law on their side?

This is the way that Shakespeare presents both sides of the question. The play, says Coleridge in one of his lectures on Shakespeare, 'illustrates the wonderfully philosophic impartiality of Shakespeare's politics'. This has been taken by some critics to mean that Shakespeare, in his plays at least, has no politics. Thus John Dover Wilson, in the Cambridge edition of *Coriolanus*, scoffs at attempts to draw parallels between the play and modern political alignments. For Wilson, the absurdity is demonstrated by the fact that the play has, on different occasions, prompted both left- and right-wing interpretations. He concludes that 'In *Coriolanus*, as in his other plays, Shakespeare is interested in dramatic art and nothing else'. This is really to cut Shakespeare down to size. But more than that, what he fails to allow is that to argue thus is just as much a political response as to read the play in Marxist or fascist terms.

That Shakespearean double-sidedness, his ability to present both sides of a question sympathetically, is where his political strength lies. His method is not to coach people into a particular viewpoint but to confront them with a problem, a set of contradictions. He contrives no solutions, but forces his audience to think, to grapple with the problem for themselves. And that is the most subversively political approach of all.

4.4 JACOBEAN TOPICALITY

Other topical issues of the play beyond the broad political picture would be the popular uprisings, reflecting those which had punctuated the English scene from the last years of Elizabeth's reign. The 1607 grain riots would have provided an immediate parallel, occurring perhaps just months before the play's first appearance; and it is notable that the several popular grievances recorded in Plutarch are reduced by Shakespeare to the topical one of food shortages.

The class conflict which underlay the disputes between King and Parliament could become brutally forthright in these riots. In the Oxfordshire rising of 1597 there was talk of disposing of the gentry. Those who flaunted wealth and position were doing nothing to dampen down the situation. Sermons are a useful index to current concerns, and in 1595 we find William Burton preaching against the insolence of those who, acquiring fine property, 'or a velvet coat upon their backs', treat their poor neighbours 'but as peasants and slaves'. Not that Burton is in any sense a liberal. He is as reactionary as Shakespeare's Roman patricians, exercised not over the misfortunes of the poor but over the danger of provoking them to riot. He approves – sees as divinely appointed – what the play exposes to criticism: the patricians' use of others' poverty 'as an inventory to particularise their abundance' (I.i.20).

However, Shakespeare was not alone in viewing the issue in less narrow terms. In particular, the problem of the lower orders having no constitutional voice by which to express grievances was addressed by various writers. Sir Philip Sidney shows how this must inevitably lead to civil disturbances. In a rapidly changing society pressure was building for commensurate constitutional changes.

Shakespeare is perhaps attempting to peer into the future when he presents a franchised citizenry. Serious attempts in this direction were to be made some decades on during the Civil War. But they were thwarted, just as Shakespeare's patricians seek to thwart the results of social progress by keeping the people in ignorance of how to exercise their constitutional power. On the other side, the Tribunes seek to mould them into a political force and the inevitable result is conflict.

The English social revolution has its counterpart in the play's opposition between materialism and militarism. Materialism is frequently attacked on the Jacobean stage as a major social ill. But the problem it poses is not a simple one. Coriolanus has imbibed his mother's patrician contempt for 'woollen vassals, things created/To buy and sell with groats' (III.ii.9–10). And he abhors the prospects of going to the market-place, where he must sell himself like a harlot (III.ii.112, 131). To behave thus is to be placed on the demeaning level of one who works, as distinct from one who takes the profits of work.

But Shakespeare himself was a beneficiary of this new materialism, without which the masses would have continued to live on a knife-edge between subsistence and starvation. And is the trade of the market-place so inferior to the aristocratic trade of the sword? James I's diplomatic efforts did much to devalue the latter, not least in 1604 when he arranged a peace settlement between England and Spain after years of hostility between the two countries. Some of his subjects remained restive. The puritan divine John Barlow preached seriously the argument which Shakespeare presents ironically in IV.v. In this time of peace, Barlow asserts, our valiant men are grown fat and pursy (short winded). And he speaks of their weapons in terms which symbolise an overall social degeneracy: 'The spiders have woven webs in our helmets and head-pieces; the worms eat into the very heart and pith of our shafts and spears'. Barlow probably began preaching this, his favourite sermon, several years after the appearance of Shakespeare's play. Periods of extended peace are apt to breed such notions. It is interesting to find Tennyson, in his monodrama *Maud*, responding to the outbreak of the Crimean War in much the same imagery. Forty years of peace in Europe are summed up in figures of 'the cobweb woven across the cannon's throat' or the cannon-ball rusting 'on a slothful shore'.

But James, in his peace diplomacy, has created a new climate in which Shakespeare can explore the moral status of heroes and heroism more radically than ever. He demonstrates through Coriolanus himself that true courage is a moral quality far above battlefield valour.

4.5 THE PRESENT RELEVANCE OF *CORIOLANUS*

It is sometimes suggested that Shakespeare's creative genius lies in his ability to stand outside the common assumptions of his own day and write for all time. But not even Shakespeare could manage that. We have only to consider one formal aspect – his heavy dependence on blank verse – to realise how far the very medium he employed differs from those favoured by present-day dramatists. Nor is there any guarantee that he will remain meaningful for future generations, unless we subscribe to the doctrine of the unchanging human heart.

What may be urged with confidence, since it is readily demonstrable, is that Shakespeare has much to say to us. But even the relative importance of his plays alters, not to say their meaning, with changing socio-political circumstances. These are the terms in which we may account for periods of accentuated interest in *Coriolanus*, such as that presently enjoyed by the play. What it represents is a marked shift of attention on Shakespeare's part from the role of ruler to that of citizen. This chimes well enough with the modern democratised viewpoint and with current scepticism about notions of greatness. Recent history has taught us to beware of unaccountable rule, of too much power falling into the hands of individuals.

If Shakespeare's play is not an advocation of democracy, it certainly exposes some of the dangers for which democracy is one partial solution. And the terms in which it addresses the dangers of glorifying war are as relevant to the late twentieth century as they were to the early seventeenth.

But a writer's importance depends not only on his dealing with subjects that matter, but on his giving them penetrating expression. His mode of expression is part of the meaning. It is necessary to insist on the primacy of meaning because there are still those who seem to suppose that response to Shakespeare's dramatic verse is a matter of gushes and palpitations.

Shakespeare's quality is not indefinable. Sharpness and depth of perception are articulated within and subordinated to the dramatic structure. The present play is particularly well crafted, with no incidental brilliances: everything has its place in the organic development of the action. So the quotations game, much used to represent Shakespeare as a purveyor of suitable orthodoxies, offers only wild distortion. There is a London statue, erected during the last century in memory of Sir John Burgoyne who died in 1871. He was an eminent soldier, and his achievement is summed up in lines from *Coriolanus*:

> How youngly he began to serve his country,
> How long continued . . . (II.iii.234–5)

Restored to their context, these lines would be a great deal less flattering than those responsible for the statue's erection must have intended. In any case, it is odd to associate a national hero with a figure most notable for betraying his country.

But this exemplifies a deplorable tendency which is tied up with the idea of Shakespeare's classic status. It is reductive to ignore the fact that Shakespeare was writing as an Elizabethan. It is still more reductive to treat him as if what he is offering is a collection of wise saws or readily detachable quotations.

We should forget that Shakespeare is a 'great' writer, a classic, a safe bet for education curricula. He is a dangerous writer, as much challenging as sustaining received ideas. He writes with great sympathy, but also with a sharp critical intelligence. When we approach him we should have our own critical intelligence working at full power.

5 DRAMATIC TECHNIQUES

5.1 TRAGIC SHAPE

> Some say that it is a political treatise, some that it is not: some say
> that Shakespeare was on the side of Coriolanus in his contempt for
> the people; others deny it. Others again see the centre of the drama
> in the relationship between a man of action and the mother who is
> responsible for his faults and his virtues.

The above quotation is from a review by Alan Pryce-Jones of
Olivier's second *Coriolanus* at Stratford (*Observer*, 12 July 1959).
This play, like any art-work, retains its hold on us precisely by being
endlessly debatable. Meaning is provisional, not fixed: it changes
with our changing circumstances. This is especially apparent in the
critical pendulum-swinging between personal and political interpretations.

These elements in the play make opposing demands. Clearly
Coriolanus has a major place in Shakespeare's scheme. As individual
he towers head and shoulders above everyone else. Even during that
long stretch of 162 lines at the start of the play we are made very much
aware of him, greedy for his first appearance. But if Shakespeare had
been intent only on arousing expectations in this way, he could have
achieved his end far more succinctly. What engages him just as much
here is the exposition of that class conflict which runs throughout the
play. He is evidently much interested in his ill-used citizens, and their
demands for government representation.

Political interests seem to give way to the personal in the last acts;
but Coriolanus is a somewhat doubtful tragic hero. His obvious
heroics, or his martyrdom 'to the aristocratic idea' (Middleton
Murry), are of only limited appeal. Nor is he notably attractive,
though his behaviour is much less vicious than Macbeth's. But

Macbeth is introspective, inwardly racked by his misdeeds. We can involve ourselves with the tortured spirit of the man if not with his grosser actions. But there is little of this in Coriolanus, who is not given to self-laceration.

To set him in suitably tragic isolation, and thereby render him sympathetic, it is necessary to detach him from the patrician group; to show him as the military man who characteristically exists within a society yet is not governed by its rules. By virtue of his function he must enjoy extraordinary dispensations, so feels the fury of betrayal at being brought to an ordinary accounting.

But if we proceed thus, if we seek too wholeheartedly to shape him into the sympathetic tragic hero, it can only be at the expense of other elements in the play. It is often recognised that this is just as much Rome's tragedy, or that of the citizens, as it is Coriolanus's. In other words we should not identify with Coriolanus in the way that we might with other of Shakespeare's tragic heroes.

In this way, then – and it is a critical commonplace – Shakespeare has radically altered his tragic design. This is not to say that we should resolutely withhold sympathy from Coriolanus. It would be hard to do so, for instance, in IV.iv and V.iii. But what the play achieves is a remarkable spread of sympathy. There is no single angle of vision. If the citizens are right in their political aims, Coriolanus is not simply wrong. We are made continually aware of the complexity of human behaviour in both public and private sectors. Coriolanus himself may not have the complexity of Hamlet or Macbeth, but nor does he dominate the play in the style that they do. Overall, *Coriolanus* is no less profound than those other tragedies.

The actor Francis Gentleman, in 1774, put forward what was to harden into critical cliché when he suggested that the embassy of women forms the play's climax, and that thereafter interest dwindles. But the Roman scenes, both before and during the return of the women, develop out of the scene of confrontation with Coriolanus, as a natural and necessary sequel to it. The first of these works, intensely and ironically, to disclose political stresses and Coriolanus's continuing part in them as catalyst, even though he has yielded to Volumnia.

Nor does the fact that his death achieves no resolution diminish the dramatic effect. Whether the play is tragedy or debate is frequently discussed. What we see enacted is tragedy, but it contains all the materials for debate. The debate is not enacted before us but must take place in our minds; and it is intended to continue long after the actors have finished their stint. A tidier, or more embracing, conclusion would only have stood in the way of any such continuing process.

Drama works as confrontation: the audience is confronted with itself not only in Coriolanus's intransigence but in the temporising inadequacies of Menenius's politics. It all adds up to a doggedly entrenched class conflict which must have been very familiar to Shakespeare's original audiences. The greater immediacy of the Shakespearean theatre as compared with our own would have served to enforce recognition that what those audiences were watching was nothing but their own predicament. There was none of that sharp cut-off between life on stage and that amongst the audience which occurs today; no dropping of a curtain or switching on of house-lights to break the spell and catapult the audience into another dimension.

But more than prompting recognition, the play prompts a more dynamic response. Audience and actors enjoyed an intimacy of relationship seldom possible under modern conditions, so that the invented world and that of actuality merged easily. Shakespeare exploits this to achieve a carry-over between stage action and that taking place beyond the confines of the Globe Theatre. The Globe itself symbolises the process. 'All the world's a stage' was a cliché of the time, and over the performance would have fluttered the theatre's Hercules banner with its Latin motto 'The whole world stirs the actor'. Since theatrical conditions already conspired to spill the drama beyond the confines of the stage, it was so much easier for it to push on into the world outside the theatre. Hence, if there is no resolution within the play, the latter supplies the material and momentum for a continuing debate: audience participation on the grand scale. With luck it would stimulate a larger resolution, or at least increased understanding, in Shakespeare's own divided society.

5.2 LANGUAGE AND STRUCTURE

Although Shakespeare's chief medium in the play is blank verse, it is notable that almost a quarter of the text is written in prose. This contrasts with the insignificant use of prose in both *Julius Caesar* and *Antony and Cleopatra*. Amongst the tragedies, only *Hamlet* and *King Lear* rely so lavishly on prose. The reason for Shakespeare's writing so much of *Coriolanus* in prose is not far to seek. He follows a convention whereby the lower orders are apt to express themselves in prose. Since Shakespeare is especially interested here in what Lear describes as 'unaccommodated man', the high incidence of prose is partly explained.

But Shakespeare also demonstrates a flexible relationship between the rhythms of verse and prose. Passages of North's Plutarch are absorbed easily into Shakespearean pentameters. But a scene wholly original to Shakespeare, that introducing the women of Coriolanus's household (I.iii), is rendered largely in plangent prose. Menenius too, as a reflex of his bridging role between plebeian and patrician, moves fluently between verse and prose.

In the speech to the Tribunes in which Menenius refers to himself as 'a humorous [whimsical] patrician' (II.i.46), characteristic features occur. His bonhomie and this reminder of his reputation for whimsy give him licence to be thoroughly insulting to the Tribunes whilst still retaining their goodwill. 'I cannot call you Lycurguses', he scoffs. The play is not overloaded with allusive reference, and some which occur are designed (as here) to separate off the educated speaker from his auditors. Lycurgus, the notorious Spartan legislator, was ruthlessly authoritarian, so Menenius's gibe perhaps falls a little flat in view of the Tribunes' quite different convictions. But he plays a similar game with the phrase 'your bisson conspectuities', where his opaque way of referring to what he considers to be the Tribunes' blind vision adds another dimension of rudeness: these Tribunes are here plainly Elizabethans, deemed lacking in the education necessary to elucidate Menenius's Latin-based coinage.

There is something comparable in Coriolanus's sarcastically dismissive 'acclamations hyperbolical' (I.ix.50) as the troops salute his prowess in the field. The scornful phrases recur as he disputes with the Tribunes: 'this bosom multiplied', 'The multitudinous tongue' (III.i.130, 155). Polysyllabics are used sparingly in the play. They are the more effective for being set amongst words of one or two syllables:

> Rome must know
> The value of her own. 'Twere a concealment
> Worse than a theft, no less than a traducement,
> To hide your doings. (I.ix.20–3)

As here, these lengthy words frequently relate to Coriolanus or his activities; indeed, his newly-won name means an increase of several syllables over his original one.

Time and again speeches begin in mid-line, cutting right across the verse structure. On the page at least they symbolise the harsh divisions which operate in the social and political worlds of the play. Again, the argument between Coriolanus and the Tribunes supplies a good example, one working in combination with Shakespeare's apt use of metrical discords:

CORIOLANUS: I say they nourish'd disobedience, fed
The ruin of the state.
BRUTUS: Why shall the people give
One that speaks thus their voice?
CORIOLANUS: I'll give my reasons
More worthier than their voices. (III.i.116–19)

If the even beat of the iambic pentameter may be taken to represent social harmony, then the jerkiness and extra feet work contrapuntally to show the breakdown of that harmony. Thus social dislocations and incompatibilities are woven into the very texture of the language, bitterness and hostility into the shaping of a phrase. In this way, the structure of the verse (or prose) continually reinforces tone.

If the prevailing tone is ironic – about which so much has been noted in the commentary that it would be tedious to pursue it further – a dominant structural feature is that of oppositions, of antitheses. In larger terms there are oppositions between patricians and plebs, or between Volsces and Romans. These run through the language with a pervasiveness which stifles any hope of reconciliation. Right from the outset the poorness and leanness of the citizens are set against the goodness and abundance of the patricians (I.i.14–20). Accusations of 'strong breaths' will turn to a demonstration of 'strong arms' (I.i.59–60). On a more tortuously quibbling example, 'Let us revenge this with our pikes, ere we become rakes' (I.i.21–2), the eighteenth-century commentator Edward Capell provides a good lead. He spots how the fun derives from 'the equivocal meaning of the words "pike" and "rake"'. By the one is intended 'the military . . . pike and the countryman's pitchfork; by the other that same countryman's rake and a person emaciated'.

Coriolanus is persistently delineated in terms of sharp oppositions or balanced contrasts.

He's poor in no one fault, but stored with all. (II.i.17)

Before him he carries noise, and behind him he leaves tears; (II.i.157–8)

You have served nobly of your country, and you have not behaved nobly. (II.iii.87–8)

        With a proud heart he wore
His humble weeds. (II.iii.151–2)

He responds in kind against those hated citizens, the 'banging about of contraries', says Granville-Barker, being 'like so many boxes on the ear':

> What would you have, you curs,
> That like not peace nor war? The one affrights you,
> The other makes you proud . . .
> You are no surer, no,
> Than is the coal of fire upon the ice,
> Or hailstone in the sun. Your virtue is,
> To make him worthy whose offence subdues him,
> And curse that justice did it. Who deserves greatness,
> Deserves your hate; and your affections are
> A sick man's appetite, who desires most that
> Which would increase his evil. (I.i.168–78)

These formulations are crude, imprecise, dangerous and divisive. Nor do they operate only on the larger political front. Coriolanus continually responds to his own predicament in the same paradoxical style: 'steel' growing 'Soft as the parasite's silk' (I.ix.44–5), or 'base tongue' against 'noble heart' (III.ii.100). He declares, 'I shall be lov'd when I am lack'd' (IV.i.15), the alliteration enforcing the paradox. And again, in banishment,

> My birthplace hate I, and my love's upon
> This enemy town. (IV.iv.23–4)

These linguistic habits point to the way that political confrontations are paralleled by oppositions in his own nature. Deficiencies in both private and public worlds of the play are exposed in this language of contradiction and conflict.

Oxymorons, contradictions in terms, are a further expression of a society deeply divided against itself. But the divisions exist within groups and individuals, too. Coriolanus cannot 'Put on the gown, stand naked' (II.ii.137); and he urges that the citizens be given no power, 'The sweet which is their poison' (III.i.156). Elsewhere, the Third Citizen uses the same figure to describe his party's disunity: 'their consent of one direct way should be at once to all the points o' th' compass' (II.iii.23–4).

The language of the play is by no means as plain as it has sometimes been made out to be. Coriolanus's opening speeches provide a great rush of metaphors, including such fully formed ones as that which perceives dependence on the plebs as swimming 'with fins of lead' (I.i.179). Sometimes it has a pithy, semi-proverbial flavour: 'The tartness of his face sours ripe grapes' (V.iv.17–18). But the movement is quick, not expansive, remarkable chiefly for forceful compression. This is a feature of both prose and verse, and is not confined to moments of urgency. Menenius is under some pressure when he exhorts the rioting citizens to identify the gods, not their early governors, as the source of their misfortunes: 'Your knees to them, not arms, must help' (I.i.73). By this quick antithesis, 'knees' pointing the 'arms' quibble, he seeks to replace the force of weapons with devout submission. Since heavenly and earthly rulers share the pronoun 'them', they would also share this submission. Such verbal adroitness is a measure of the political skill which has so far succeeded in keeping these citizens in their place.

But it is merely Coriolanus's habitual impatience which prompts another instance of severe foreshortening, as he thanks Cominius for the gifts of horse and name:

> I mean to stride your steed, and at all times
> To undercrest your good addition,
> To th' fairness of my power (I.ix.69–71)

Pride and modesty cancel out as, superimposed on to the picture of dominant horseman comes this more tightpacked idea of undercresting. Since this relates to heraldry – 'addition' has the heraldic sense of a fresh honour added to a coat of arms – it is emblematic of everything that Coriolanus holds sacred. Beneath this newly embellished crest he will comport himself as fittingly as he is able.

Often it is the coinage like 'undercrest', or the new compound which provides the means to conciseness. The abrupt violence of Coriolanus's coming of age on the battlefield is splendidly caught in Cominius's 'His pupil age/Man – enter'd thus' (II.ii.98–9). Such devices match the whole movement of the play, which is quick, precise, inexorable.

5.3 IMAGERY

Verse and prose, then, tend to be sinewy rather than sumptuous. Right at the centre is Rome itself. Charles Knight, a mid-nineteenth-century editor of Shakespeare, went so far as to declare that the hero of Shakespeare's Roman trilogy, *Julius Caesar*, *Antony and Cleopatra* and *Coriolanus*, is the city itself.

Whatever reservations we might have about that, there is no denying that, in the present play, the urban setting is realised with concrete immediacy. From IV.vi onwards, the imagery is of a burning city, its smoke-pall hanging over the action as an almost palpable threat (Bradley, *A Miscellany*, p. 104). But even that imagery which reeks of destruction helps to form the city in our minds. We hear of the melting of 'the city leads' (IV.vi.83), or Cominius's

> That is the way to lay the city flat,
> To bring the roof to the foundation,
> And bury all which yet distinctly ranges
> In heaps and piles of ruin. (III.i.202–5)

Further, we are made vividly aware of the kind of society, divided and faction-ridden, which exists within these walls. These social divisions provide the dramatic mainspring. Patterns of recurrent imagery highlight those incompatibilities of interest which only disappear in time of war. War is a great simplifier of issues but, once peace is established, factional interests reassert themselves.

Animal imagery is crudely expressive of these. The first thing we hear of Coriolanus is that he is 'a very dog' (I.i.27); and when he appears on the scene he describes the citizens as 'curs' (167). Where they should be found lions, they are hares, and 'Where foxes, geese' (170–1). They are mice afraid of the cat (I.vi.44), or crows asserting themselves against eagles (III.i.138). Later, Coriolanus is the sea eagle, the osprey, and the Romans his fishy prey (IV.vii.34). This pairing has been seen to accord with the play's view of the inborn inequality of men. But Shakespeare offers a more complex picture. Hence the citizens are not always associated with feeble and cowardly creatures, nor is Coriolanus always the regal animal. The many-headed hydra will repeatedly signify the citizens (II.iii.16; III.i.92; IV.i.1), while Coriolanus becomes a dragon (IV.i.30; IV.vii.23; V.iv.13).

Nor is the triter viewpoint supported by that image of Coriolanus as a chick 'cluck'd . . . to the wars', by his hen-mother (V.iii.163). This image is not like Menenius's absurd pretence that Coriolanus is a bear 'that lives like a lamb' (II.i.11). It is to be taken seriously. Strength and weakness blur together in a morally confusing way. Coriolanus's dignity survives only because of the genuine love which the image expresses. Heroes may be men like other men, but at least that means they can love and be loved like other men.

Closely associated with the abusive animal imagery is that of sickness. The people's disaffection is conceived as a sore: they rub the poor itch of their opinions and make themselves scabs (I.i.164–5).

But we are already aware that there are deeper wounds in this body politic. Later, Coriolanus is said to be 'a disease that must be cut away', though Menenius declares that it is curable (III.i.292–4). This points to the relationship between a diseased society and the warp in Coriolanus's personality. In just the same way, social and personal coalesce in those nightmare visions of melting roofs and collapsing walls. Since Coriolanus himself invites us to identify him with Rome, these are images of self-destruction, too.

Menenius has some notion, however imperfect, of the problem. He suspects that at least a show of humility by Coriolanus might provide 'physic/For the whole state' (III.ii.33–4). But his way is not to grapple with root causes, but to have difficulties 'patch'd/With cloth of any colour' (III.i.250–1). A case in point is his belly-fable, which the citizens have no difficulty in seeing to be double-edged. Accusations against the patrician belly as 'idle and unactive' (I.i.98) clearly have some basis. The community of interests which the fable purports to illustrate has no existence in a society which sharply divides into 'haves' and 'have nots'. This is ironically affirmed through the boorishness of addressing hungry men with a belly-fable.

The fable ties together imagery of social disease and that of food. Harry Levin, in 'An Introduction to *Coriolanus*', notes a further ironic merging as 'battle is described as if it were harvest, with the swords of destruction figuratively turning into the ploughshares of fertility' (I.iii.35–7). This interlocking of the different spheres of imagery is achieved with sophisticated precision, just one aspect of the structural mastery shown in this play.

5.4 CHARACTERS

The Roman Citizens

There are two protagonists: Coriolanus himself and the Roman citizenry. There are, of course, notable secondary characters. But none of them is, by himself, an adequate counterpoise to Coriolanus. Only the citizens, in their collective identity, have the necessary weight; though it is to be noted that they exist not only as a group but are realised, several of them, as interesting individuals. Both aspects, the collective and the individual, are important not only in terms of dramatic tension and equation but also in their thematic bearing. It is precisely because the citizens are disregarded as individuals by their social superiors that they become a collective threat to the status quo. Only as a group can they make any political impact, and then only by unconstitutional means, since, until their rioting forces the creation of a tribunate, they have no constitutional voice.

We see how a reluctant rioter, the Second Citizen, may harden decisively through contact with members of the governing class; or how a show of camaraderie from social superiors will remove the edge of the people's resentment. This was nicely symbolised in the première of Brecht's version of the play in 1962. The citizens were engaged in a sit-down strike. Menenius's haranguing was ignored until he slowly sat down among them to recite his belly-fable. That they are imposed on in this way is due not to stupidity but social conditioning. Nor should we accept the patrician evaluation of them. A. C. Bradley deals with one insult they receive by asking: 'If they were cowards, how could Rome be standing where we see it stands?'.

Volumnia

Chief among the secondary characters are Volumnia, Aufidius and Menenius. Volumnia personifies a certain kind of Roman matron, ruthless in her determination yet not without political cunning. She knows how to touch Coriolanus's pride as well as appealing to his filial piety. MacCallum (*Shakespeare's Roman Plays*, p. 549), offers a pithy summing up: 'The passion of maternity, whether interpreted as maternal love or as maternal pride, penetrates her nature to the core, not, however, to melt but to harden it'. Wilson Knight (*The Imperial Theme*, p. 190) remarks this strange emotional confusion, in which she 'objectifies [Coriolanus's] honour and glory as a thing to love beyond himself', creating in the process 'an idiot robot, a creaky clockwork giant; a stone Colossus whose tread will be heavy on his compatriots' bodies'. But he discovers a more genuine love there, too, in those lines where she describes herself as

> poor hen, fond of no second brood, [who]
> Has cluck'd thee to the wars and safely home,
> Loaden with honour. (V.iii.162–4)

This 'lovely image throws back light on years of devotion, pathetic unwisdom of all-too-natural mother love' (p. 195). None the less, Coriolanus is destroyed by acting out his mother's fantasies of masculinity.

Aufidius

The relationship between Coriolanus and Aufidius also has that dangerous preoccupation with honour threaded into it. Aufidius is

Coriolanus's chief rival on the battlefield, though the latter maintains a comfortable ascendancy in that sector. But Aufidius finds compensation in a far greater political astuteness. If man-to-man confrontations lead only to humiliation, he will turn to intrigue. He is a cruder version of Coriolanus; his nature, too, though in different terms, is finely balanced between heroism (that most slippery of virtues) and treachery. His hospitable welcome, when Coriolanus arrives so unexpectedly at his house, parallels the Roman's more generous side. His initial delight in the idea of entering into partnership with Coriolanus is not unlike the latter's willingness to follow Cominius. But in the long run neither is prepared to renounce honours, even if the drives of ambition lie dormant for a time. The similarities between the two are clear enough, then. But Aufidius's smouldering envy, his most interesting aspect, has no clear counterpart in Coriolanus. Further, there are depths to Coriolanus which do not show up in Aufidius: the reverence exhibited towards his mother or tenderness to his wife; or that curious vein of irony which is exposed on Coriolanus's arrival amongst the Volscians after his banishment. Aufidius is eventually a foil, his relationship to Coriolanus defining his real significance for us.

Menenius

Menenius has a capacity for irony, though it is of a sly kind which intermittently betrays his humane pretensions. He offers the perfect contrast to Coriolanus, being bent on indolent pleasures rather than fame and glory. Yet at bottom their political outlooks are identical, however different their objectives and modes of approach. Coriolanus's choler is matched by an easy pliancy in Menenius. He knows that to bend is not to break. He is the most persuasive talker in the play, able to sway the people while granting no concessions. So he is no-one's fool.

He is also what Maynard Mack would call the primary foil for Coriolanus. Mack ('The Jacobean Shakespeare', *Jacobean Theatre*, London: Stratford Upon Avon Studies I, 1960, p. 20) sees the relationship between Coriolanus and Menenius to be of a kind found frequently in the drama from classical times onwards. The relationship offers a duality of outlook, the Menenius role providing a mouthpiece for the values of community and that of Coriolanus for the passionate life of the individual. 'What matters to the community is obviously accommodation – all those adjustments and resiliences that enable it to survive; whereas what matters to the individual, at least in his heroic moods, is just as obviously integrity – all that enables him to remain an *individual*, one thing not many.'

But once we have recognised the archetype, what most engages our attention are those particularities which cause this pair to deviate from the norm. For neither Coriolanus's integrity nor Menenius's sense of community are to be taken at quite face value. The eighteenth-century critic John Dennis took Menenius to be a buffoon. But Middleton Murry (*Countries of the Mind*, p. 19) registers his cynicism. And in 1964, R. F. Hill ('"Coriolanus": Violentest Contrariety', *Essays and Studies*, 17, p. 19) went so far as to describe him baring 'the fangs of his prejudice' at the Tribunes.

But the preponderant view lies between the two. It is summed up in that avuncular affability which Leo McKern brought to the role in the 1963 production at Nottingham. This has far-reaching consequences. Once concede that there is anything in the Murry-Hill view – Granville-Barker also found him thoroughly unsympathetic (*Preface to Coriolanus*, p. 6) – and it undermines Kenneth Burke's argument that Coriolanus must be viewed as a *bona fide* hero since '*every* person of good standing in the play admires him or loves him and is loyal to him, despite his excesses' ('*Coriolanus* and the Delights of Faction', *Hudson Review*, 19, 1966, p. 199). It is difficult to see why Menenius, or Volumnia for that matter, should be considered of better standing than, say, the Tribunes.

The Tribunes

Though the Tribunes are wily, there is no justification for seeing them as self-seeking. They are frequently played and described as trade union leaders. When considering the light in which they are represented by Menenius and his fellow patricians, we should keep in mind the way in which the mass media represent their modern-day equivalents. It is not those who are selling out their membership who are apt to get the bad press, but those who most actively represent the membership's interests. The same reasons hold in both cases. The Tribunes are reviled precisely because they present a threat to the existing power group. Hence, the more they are reviled by the opposition, the less reason does Shakespeare give us for viewing them as time-serving grafters. Indeed, under their guidance, the city appears briefly at its most attractive, the bustle of the market-place punctuated by song. This is a glimpse of the normal, natural life of a busy city, soon to be disrupted by Coriolanus's vicious threat.

Coriolanus

But neither is it appropriate to view Coriolanus in unrelieved terms. He is just as much at the mercy of hostile witnesses as the Tribunes, though in his case he himself provides confirmation for many of their allegations. Further, we quickly perceive that he is not only a threat to the plebs but a liability to his own kind. He may be a stalwart champion in time of war, but he is also the kind of person who, given the scope, is likely to precipitate a war. Coriolanus is violent, selfish, prideful – monstrously so, in fact, though he is not a monster. If he is a monster to the citizens, that is because they see only what affects them, his public face. That he is tender to his wife would leave them unmoved; likewise that strange moment when, still covered in the blood and sweat of battle, he spares a thought for a prisoner, a poor man who had shown him kindness in Corioli (I.ix.80–2). The effect is marred since he cannot recall the man's name in order to have him released. But Shakespeare has attached particular meaning to the episode which, in the source, concerned a wealthy prisoner of the Volsces, an old friend of Coriolanus's. This latter episode may be taken to symbolise Coriolanus's unrealised or perverted potential. His dalliance with politics shows up better than anything else the radical difference between himself and his fellow patricians. They, not least his mother, are fully prepared to sell themselves for political advantage. That he is prevailed upon to follow suit is an indication of weakness. But his extreme discomfort in the role of politican shows the impossibility of his ever becoming reconciled to the habits and behaviour of his peers.

The vulgar or negative side of this difference is manifested in his pride. More positively it shows up in his integrity. But integrity, although it has become entangled with notions of moral uprightness, has more strictly to do with that seamless consistency of behaviour which, though morally neutral, in Coriolanus leads to violence and disaster.

As we have noted, Coriolanus's integrity slips at times, under pressure from his mother. But that is a lesser matter. The real trouble lies in the fact that his integrity, however admirable it may look when set against the wheeling and dealing of his fellow patricians, is dedicated to no very healthy social outlook. He is not only out of harmony with his peers, but with the rest of Roman society. Even so, while Coriolanus is isolated in some respects from his peers from the outset, he is still on terms of friendship and respect until he chooses to break them off. His brand of integrity and their politics may not mix, but this in no way allows him to enjoy a more socially responsive and responsible role than they. He shares all their class prejudices and his integrity merely prevents him from disguising them in the interests of social cohesion. It is an integrity which denies integration. So his isolation runs deep, translating as spiritual impoverishment. He has strong family ties but no sense of larger community obligation.

If social conscience were a factor in elections to senatorial office, it would be hard to imagine a less suitable candidate than Coriolanus. But the real qualifications are birth and social position, and his prowess at manslaughter provides a useful bonus. Speaking to the Tribunes, Menenius says of Coriolanus on his behalf:

> He loves your people,
> But tie him not to be their bedfellow. (II.ii.64–5)

It is doubtful whether this could be truthfully said of any of the patricians; it is ludicrously inappropriate to Coriolanus. Yet it is the correct prescription if this society is to be restored to health, nicely distinguishing between rights and obligations. The ruling class has a right to choose its intimates; it has an obligation to look after the underprivileged. But nice distinctions are part of Menenius's stock-in-trade when dealing with the Tribunes. He plays the hypocrite in a way that would be unthinkable for Coriolanus. It is the latter's tragedy that while he has the stature to reject the mere *appearance* of a full social involvement, he is incapable of shaking off that conditioning which makes him scorn the *reality*.

6 SPECIMEN PASSAGE
AND ANALYSIS

COMINIUS:
> the deeds of Coriolanus
Should not be utter'd feebly. It is held
That valour is the chiefest virtue and
Most dignifies the haver: if it be,
The man I speak of cannot in the world
Be singly counter-pois'd. At sixteen years,
When Tarquin made a head for Rome, he fought
Beyond the mark of others; our then dictator,
Whom with all praise I point at, saw him fight,
When with his Amazonian chin he drove
The bristled lips before him; he bestrid
An o'erpress'd Roman, and i'th'consul's view
Slew three opposers; Tarquin's self he met
And struck him on his knee. In that day's feats,
When he might act the woman in the scene,
He prov'd best man i'th'field, and for his meed
Was brow-bound with the oak. His pupil age
Man-enter'd thus, he waxed like a sea,
And in the brunt of seventeen battles since
He lurch'd all swords of the garland. For this last,
Before and in Corioles, let me say
I cannot speak him home. He stopp'd the fliers,
And by his rare example made the coward
Turn terror into sport; as weeds before
A vessel under sail, so men obey'd
And fell below his stem: his sword, death's stamp,
Where it did mark, it took; from face to foot
He was a thing of blood, whose every motion
Was tim'd with dying cries: alone he enter'd

The mortal gate of th'city, which he painted
With shunless destiny, aidless came off,
And with a sudden reinforcement struck
Corioles like a planet. Now all's his;
When by and by the din of war 'gan pierce
His ready sense, then straight his doubled spirit
Requicken'd what in flesh was fatigate,
And to the battle came he, where he did
Run reeking o'er the lives of men, as if
'Twere a perpetual spoil; and till we call'd
Both field and city ours, he never stood
To ease his breast with panting,
    . . . Our spoils he kick'd at,
And look'd upon things precious as they were
The common muck of the world. He covets less
Than misery itself would give, rewards
His deeds with doing them, and is content
To spend the time to end it. (II.ii.82–129)

The Senate has met in order to hear from Cominius, commanding general against the Volsces, of Coriolanus's valour and contribution to victory. He is invited to speak at length by one of the senators, though the Tribunes voice uncertain reservations. For this is no mere military report but an election speech on behalf of Coriolanus. The latter, finding the prospect of hearing himself praised distasteful, leaves the chamber. Cominius's eulogy, for such it is, has its effect on the Senate. They, says Menenius on Coriolanus's return, 'are well pleas'd/To make thee consul' (132–3).

The speech has a key place in the play, not only shedding important light on Coriolanus's character but making a major contribution to Shakespeare's critical re-evaluation of greatness. The speech is concerned with Coriolanus's military virtue, the context in which his immediate claim to greatness must lie. Indeed, Cominius begins with a Roman orthodoxy whereby 'valour is the chiefest virtue and/Most dignifies the haver' (83–5). Coriolanus has dignity of this particular kind, though the whole tenor of the play undercuts belief in valour as 'the chiefest virtue'. But, however it is to be rated, Cominius urges that for valour Coriolanus has no equal ('cannot in the world/Be singly counter-pois'd', 86–7). He was blooded in the overthrow of Tarquin – last of the Roman kings – whom he actually wounded (88–9, 95). Although at the time a mere stripling of sixteen, he was a match for more mature fighters: 'with his Amazonian chin he drove/The bristled lips before him' (91–2). Lacking masculine facial hair, he had the fighting spirit of those warrior women; and all this before his voice had broken while he might still have been playing softer women's roles on a stage which debarred actresses. In this image, as so often, ancient Rome and Elizabethan London merge. Here 'act the woman' and 'prov'd [the] man' (95–7) provides a characteristic antithesis. And equally characteristic is the forceful compression used to suggest this precipitate coming of age in battle, as Cominius brings his recital up to date:

> His pupil age
> Man-enter'd thus, he waxed like a sea,
> And in the brunt of seventeen battles since
> He lurch'd all swords of the garland. (98–101)

The sea simile tentatively anticipates a whole series of images in the speech which contrives to dehumanise Coriolanus. For the moment the stress is on the ascendancy which he achieved and maintained through many campaigns: 'swords' = swordsmen, from whom Shakespeare has him win the garland as the best man in the field.

Cominius cannot do justice to Coriolanus's recent exploits, when his effect on morale was electric:

> He stopp'd the fliers,
> And by his rare example made the coward
> Turn terror into sport. (103–5)

Yet this was manifestly not sport, but bloody murder. Such a response is not inappropriate. Shakespeare ensures that we take the point by what follows (105–14). Coriolanus is irresistible, inexorable. There is no humanity in the picture. He is likened to a vessel cutting through the weeds, not of its own volition but through the outside force of the wind. The language is compressed in a way that yields ambiguities, but they are fruitful ones. Thus we might distinguish the men who obeyed from those who 'fell before his stem' (106–7), identifying the former with the 'fliers' and 'cowards'. But, more subtly, both terms may apply to Coriolanus's opponents, who fall as if obedient to a superior will rather than cut down by a superior physical force. This accords with Aufidius's likening of Coriolanus to the osprey, who catches fish 'By sovereignty of nature' (IV.vii.35). According to folklore, the fish have an instinctive fear of the bird and turn on their backs submissive to his will. But if Coriolanus has depended on superior will, the physical force is there, too, in that iron stem, which is both the vessel's prow and his sharp sword. He is machine-like, his sword 'death's stamp' (107) – imparting death as a die-stamp makes its impression mindlessly, repetitively. Yet it is he, not just the sword, who achieves the inhuman rhythms of slaughter – his 'every motion . . . tim'd with dying cries' (109–10).

When he forces his way into Corioli, it is as if the gate becomes mortal while he turns inanimate, that 'thing of blood' (109). The gate should mean death to this lone warrior, but instead becomes death to countless others. It is a tomb for them which he paints in blood. This notion of blood-spattered walls is compressed into the figure of destiny's malign instrument which 'struck/Corioles like a planet' (113–14). The allusion is astrological. His effect on the town is malignant, like that of a planet in a hostile aspect. Nor is he satisfied with this single-handed assault, but seems refreshed by the 'din of war' (115) to

> Run reeking o'er the lives of men, as if
> 'Twere a perpetual spoil. (119–20)

He reeks of blood, his zest for slaughter seemingly inexhaustible. Nor is he indifferent to 'spoil' though, for him, it means a pure, purposeless joy in bloodletting. A few lines on, Cominius recalls how

> Our spoils he kick'd at,
> And look'd upon things precious as they were
> The common muck of the world. (124–6)

What he would represent as a virtue is undercut by Shakespeare's wordplay. Coriolanus might spurn the material benefits available to the victor on the battlefield. But is the lust for profit more degraded than the lust for killing?

When Coriolanus's killing propensity is turning against himself, Cominius begins to reappraise (IV.vi.96–6). But for the moment he invites the admiration of his auditors for a picture of inordinate valour. Or, at least, that is the usual interpretation. Under Terry Hands's direction, Geffery Dench, in the 1977 Stratford production, made Cominius deliver the speech not as eulogy but as appalling indictment. The problem with this is not that it violates our understanding of Cominius's relationship with Coriolanus. The speech is essentially choric rather than an expression of Cominius's personal attitudes. (The play offers numerous examples of such sophisticated choric comment.) But what gets lost in such an interpretation is that discrepancy between the responses of stage and theatre audiences which is needed to point up the suspect values of the Roman governing class. This is one clear function of the speech; our disquiet deepens in proportion to the Senate's growing enthusiasm. Beyond this, it controls our response to Coriolanus in the crucial episode which follows as he is recalled and tries to evade the custom of addressing the people.

A Coriolanus conceived wholly in the terms of Cominius's speech would be beyond tragic repair. The man who re-enters the Senate chamber is a different proposition, more human, more vulnerable. But there is an undeniable truth about Cominius's picture which cannot be evaded. Those strictly Roman virtues which allow Coriolanus to shine on the battlefield cannot be adapted to a civic function, despite the Senate's belief that they can.

Here is a powerful indictment, then, but not just of Coriolanus. Virgilia alone, among the Roman elite, stands for a contradictory viewpoint, one which is surely being offered for our approval. Shakespeare, writing in a climate induced by King James the peacemaker (see 4.4), is pointing up the contrast between Roman attitudes and those of his own day. At least when Aufidius's serving-men expound values consonant with those of Cominius in IV.v, they have their tongues set firmly in their cheeks. But Rome's rulers are totally wedded to the militarist viewpoint. For them Coriolanus embodies that Roman ideal of hard, sober manliness which created a great empire. But he offers the clearest demonstration of its frighteningly destructive side, too.

7 STAGE HISTORY AND CRITICAL RECEPTION

7.1 STAGE HISTORY

Although there is no history of any performance of *Coriolanus* prior to the closing of the theatres at the time of the Civil War, the text of the play shows signs of careful preparation for the stage. Stage directions, for instance, are unusually full, and it has been plausibly suggested that this may indicate that Shakespeare was sending the script from Stratford for a colleague to produce.

In 1681, Nahum Tate brought out his own version, a follow-up to his happy-ending *King Lear*. The bias of this adaptation, *The Ingratitude of a Commonwealth, or The Fall of Coriolanus*, is sufficiently indicated by the title. Drawn to the play by the political content, which he considered to bear 'no small resemblence with the busy faction of our own time', he sought to draw the parallels closer still. But clearly, too, he felt that Shakespeare's play could use more sex and violence. Menenius and Coriolanus's son are both murdered; and Aufidius, fatally wounded by Coriolanus, plans to glut his last minutes by raping Virgilia in front of her dying husband. Box-office considerations are clearly paramount here. But Tate's lurid adaptation, designed to 'turn to money, what lay dead before', was a flop.

Other versions followed, but David Garrick restored authentic Shakespeare to the theatre in 1754, though he never acted the part himself. He was benefiting from that activity which, in the first half of the eighteenth century, had produced the earliest scholarly editions of Shakespeare. But the same year saw the first appearance of a hybrid, part Shakespeare and part James Thomson's blank verse *Coriolanus* (1749). Both versions were reviewed by Paul Hiffernan, who enjoyed Garrick's production as 'the most mobbing, huzzaing, shewy, boasting, drumming, fighting, trumpeting Tragedy' he had ever seen; whereas the hybrid was 'the divine but nodding Shakespeare put into his nightgown by Messire Thomson'. Despite a good deal of such adverse criticism, the Shakespeare-Thomson mixture held the stage, in varying proportions, well into the nineteenth century.

It was not one of the more popular of Shakespeare's plays during the eighteenth century, though it is interesting to note that *Antony and Cleopatra* was performed hardly at all during the period. It was John Kemble who was the first actor to become identified with the role. He played it frequently between 1789 and 1817, his sister, the celebrated Mrs Siddons, taking the part of Volumnia in the early years. Kemble's austere approach to tragedy fitted the role very well, and he chose it for his farewell to the stage in June 1817.

Kemble's example ensured that the role would be taken into the repertory of the great English tragic actors of the nineteenth century. The productions in which William Macready was involved between 1819 and 1839 are especially notable. According to Ralph Berry ('The Metamorphoses of *Coriolanus*', p. 23), his achievement was to play against 'a crowd that has ceased to be a mob and is in the process of becoming a segment of the people. It is a segment of some character and dignity: it has aspirations; and by readjusting the balance of dramatic sympathies, it makes a profound case against Coriolanus'.

Macready was unconcerned about textual authenticity, but he took elaborate care with setting. Some half century or so earlier one would have seen cannon peeping through the Volscian embrasures, and even Kemble anachronistically evoked Rome with mock-ups of Trajan's Column or the Arch of Constantine. Macready, on the other hand, showed the Palatine 'covered with thatched hovels' to indicate that this was a much earlier period of Roman history. In the spectacular battle scenes, the troops 'seemed thousands, not hundreds', and even the Senate scene was lavish with 'between one and two hundred . . . white-robed fathers'. But the huge scale was balanced by uncommon concern for detail. The senators were seated 'in triple rows round three sides of the stage, an effect of perspective being obtained by getting half-grown boys to present the more distant figures' (William Archer, *William Charles Macready*, London, 1890, 115).

Interior effects could be achieved by the same sort of approach. The scene was starlit as Macready entered solitary, muffled. Beyond, echoing his 'lonely grandeur', his 'still unextinguished light', the port and mole of Antium was dominated by a tall lighthouse. 'The pathetic effect is suddenly and startlingly increased by the intrusion of music on the air, as the door of Aufidius' house . . . opens on the left of the stage' (quoted by Alan S. Downer, *The Eminent Tragedian: W. C. Macready*, Cambridge, Mass., 1966, p. 234).

Samuel Phelps went for a more intimate approach. When he resumed the role in 1860, it is interesting to find the academic critic Henry Morley remarking the fine performance of Lewis Ball as First Citizen. Early twentieth-century productions followed in this tradition, those of 1901 with Sir Frank Benson and Sir Henry Irving having taken care to give due weight to the plebs in the political conflict. As Ralph Berry puts it (p. 34), 'The Roman plebeians co-starred with Benson and contested with Irving himself'. This was Irving's last new Shakespearean role, and by no means his best. On the other hand, Benson's production, which opened just two months before, found him returning to one of his favourite parts.

That the play had not lost its political bite was demonstrated during the inter-war years. In 1924, Robert Atkins's production at the Old Vic had a Coriolanus unable to remember his lines and a Volumnia described by Herbert Farjeon as 'a burlesque of an old lady on a flag-day' (*The Shakespearean Scene*, London, 1949, p. 112). But these were lesser considerations in a production apparently designed to expose the knavery of labour leaders. This was the period leading up to the General Strike. Farjeon applauds the production for representing the Tribunes 'as a couple of outrageous Hebraic scarecrows, fit for bonfires' – the racialism is characteristic of the era – while underlining the nobility of the patricians.

Atkins's message seems to have gone down well in the London of 1924. But opinions were divided a decade on when Piachaud mounted his production at the Comédie Française in Paris. It formed a rallying point for semi-fascist agitators and paramilitarists, so made its contribution to the fall of Daladier's radical government. Shakespeare's intention to move the play's issues outwards into the world of socio-political reality found crudely perverse realisation in these Paris riots.

By the same token, when Olivier first assumed the role at the Old Vic in 1938, with the dictators Hitler and Mussolini casting a dark shadow over Europe, it became anti-fascist propaganda. None the less, James Agate contrives to ignore that side of the production in his review, while finding Menenius's 'baiting of the Tribunes wholly delightful' (*Brief Chronicles*, London, 1943, p. 168). He would have been put to no such trouble by Iden Payne's Stratford production of 1939, which adopted a contrary response to current events: it ignored them. The play was smothered in tradition at a time when developments in Europe were proving it ever more contemporary.

The Stratford productions of 1952 and 1959 had an essential feature in common. In each case Coriolanus – Anthony Quayle and Laurence Olivier respectively – separated himself from the patricians as a member of the officer corps, a Roman Junker. The productions exploited this in similar ways; Olivier, according to Kenneth Tynan, using 'it to gain for the man an astounding degree of sympathy' (*Curtains*, London, Longman, 1961, p. 240). But the price paid for this success was a high one. It unbalanced the Shakespearean conception. Tynan found little else of interest besides the protagonist in either production. The people can only achieve a measure of sympathy at Coriolanus's expense. Militarism only remains a reasonable option if the production trivialises such moments as that beautiful send-up of the warrior ethic by Aufidius's servingmen.

Against these there was Bertolt Brecht's version of the play, first performed at Frankfurt on Main (1962), which not only offered a left-wing reading against Stratford's Tory emphasis (Tynan), but attacked the personality cult. As Brecht himself realised, however, there was no need to adapt Shakespeare's text to achieve a production which demolished the myth of irreplaceable greatness.

Next, Tyrone Guthrie's production, which opened the new Nottingham Playhouse in 1963, offered a Freudian reading in which Coriolanus and Aufidius, as Ralph Berry puts it, engaged in 'a prolonged homosexual duet'. Hints of this were carried over into Trevor Nunn's 1972 Stratford production. Derek Mahon (the *Listener*, 20 April 1972) describes how the confrontation between Coriolanus and Aufidius melted 'into a positively amorous wrestling bout'. Mahon also complains that, yet again, the Tribunes were played in accordance with the patricians' prejudiced view of them. But this production was more notable for spectacle and its view of the Volscians as tribal primitives. However mistaken, this approach did yield incidental benefits. That imagery which figures Coriolanus as god was literalised by these plumed warriors worshipping him in effigy on a golden throne: 'he does sit in gold, his eye/Red as 'twould burn Rome' (V.i.63–4). That they took him for their god was certainly an effective way of accounting for his immoderate popularity amongst the Volscians. 'He is their god', exlaims Cominius (IV.vi.91). If this be taken in a metaphoric sense, it still requires explanation. If in a literal sense, none is needed.

The ceremonial aspect, too, could achieve fine things. The women, back from their successful embassy, entered beneath the giant effigy of a wolf, the Romans' tribal totem. This underscored the way that Volumnia's values had shifted from personal pride to patriotic commitment. But the cost of that shift was shown, too. As Richard David describes it, Volumnia (Margaret Tyzack) 'acknowledged the salute with a distraught, almost frenzied gesture, her ravaged face showing no glimmer of joy, hardly of life' (*Shakespeare in the Theatre*, Cambridge University Press, 1978, p. 146).

More consistently successful was Terry Hands's production (Stratford, 1977), which Sally Beauman (*The Royal Shakespearean Company*, Oxford University Press, 1982, p. 342) found memorably disturbing for its attention to 'the fine moral and political shading of the text, allowing neither the protagonist nor the play's factions of family, patricians, plebeians, or tribunes extraneous sympathy or weight'. Since then there have been more one-sided productions at Stratford, Ontario (1981, director Brian Bedford) and the National Theatre, London (1984, director Peter Hall). In the former, all the nastiness in the play was confined to the Tribunes and their followers. In the latter, members of the cast and of the audience (at cut rates) occupied seats on stage ready to come forward to play the people. Such an odd and unpredictable array could hardly be expected to generate much loyalty in the Tribunes. In its own way it exemplified that modern tendency to reduce the play's political temperature by trivialising the plebs.

But the 1984 Coriolanus, Ian McKellen, brought some fascinating insights to the role. In this performance it was the first betrayal not the second which proved fatal to Coriolanus. As Michael Ratcliffe puts it (the *Observer*, 23 December 1984), 'grief and despair drain his face as Aufidius accepts his offer of treacherous help against Rome . . . Part of him had hoped Aufidius would say no and run him through then and there'. The situation is not unlike that of Antony in *Antony and Cleopatra*, who tries to kill himself in the high Roman fashion. Here, too, Coriolanus (or rather his second self Aufidius) can only manage the job messily, by means of assassins.

Over the last few decades, Coriolanus has ceased to be a rarity in the theatre. It has drawn some fine performances, many of its latent subtleties being splendidly revealed. The play, re-energised and transformed by each new production, has established itself as one of Shakespeare's finest achievements. Even the fact that this play, more than most, seems to induce a positive craving to present it as stark reinforcement of a particular ideology is tribute to, as well as reaction against, Shakespeare's superbly realist ambiguities.

7.2 CRITICAL RECEPTION

Only very recently has *Coriolanus* begun to claim the critical attention accorded to Shakespeare's other tragedies and Roman plays. People have not warmed to it but have been disturbed by it. John Dennis finds it disturbing that Aufidius is allowed to thrive and the Tribunes to escape punishment – not only for procuring Coriolanus's exile but for their 'indirect methods'. Contrariwise, his contemporary, Charles Gildon, who in 1710 published the first extended commentary on all Shakespeare's works, complains that the latter is too hard on the people. Nonetheless, he is obliged to admit that the plot favours their case.

He anticipates the radicalism of William Hazlitt, writing in the very different climate produced by the American and French Revolutions. Despite what he sees as Shakespeare's taste for rabble-baiting, Hazlitt views the play as an important contribution to political philosophy, and it prompts from him a powerful indictment of the 'born to rule' myth. Against this, a recent critic (Paul A. Cantor, *Shakespeare's Rome*, Cornell University Press, 1976) finds the play pointing to the inadequacy of the people to govern themselves.

It was the Romantic critics who first worked the rich vein of Shakespearean humour. Both the poet Coleridge and August Wilhelm Schlegel perceive 'Shakespeare's good-natured laugh at mobs'. For Schlegel, the people are visibly simple-minded, creating humour inseparable from the political issues. It is another German, G. G. Gervinus, who, developing Coleridge's hints, gives us the most important account of *Coriolanus* in the mid-nineteenth century. He offers two fresh insights: that the citizens are not to be judged by hostile opinion, and that Coriolanus and the Tribunes are set up in such a way that sympathy can be accorded to one party only at the direct expense of the other. For him the choice is simple since he subscribes to that Romantic idea of the supremacy of character over plot or theme which runs on to Bradley and beyond.

Yet A. C. Bradley finds the choice less simple. His 'Coriolanus' lecture, dating from 1912, is perhaps the single most important discussion of the play. He is illuminating largely because he finds it so intractable. Both hero and political conflict seem 'distasteful'. But he understands that while the 'conflict of hero and people is hopeless', it is the hero alone who pushes that between patricians and people in the same direction. Whatever the people's faults, it is only Coriolanus's presence that would prevent a constitutional development in their favour. He briefly weighs the possibility that *Coriolanus* is 'a drama of reconciliation' rather than a tragedy. It will fit into no preconceived outline of Shakespearean tragedy, and the result is a restless engagement with a play which challenges some of his most deeply rooted assumptions.

After Bradley, the play continues to be a battleground for opposing viewpoints. For G. Wilson Knight it demonstrates the power of love (*The Imperial Theme*, Methuen, reprinted 1965). And for Derek Traversi 'Coriolanus'. *Scrutiny* VI, 1937) it is a tragedy of irreconcilables, where 'factions are set in an iron social framework which permits no . . . community of interests'. He strangely ignores the Coleridge school in claiming that 'everyone admits [that] the people are weak, worthless and brutal'. John Palmer (*Political Characters of Shakespeare*, Macmillan, 1945) offers a scene-by-scene rebuttal of the widely held view that the Tribunes are the villains of the piece. A. P. Rossiter's basic premise (*Angel With Horns*, Longman, 1961) is that Coriolanus is Shakespeare's political spokesman, although he seeks to distinguish between Coriolanus's unpleasant character and his authorially approved convictions.

Recent lively interest in the play reflects current taste for sinewy debate rather than heady poetry or flamboyant character. In the process, Hazlitt's contention that its very poetic form is in alliance with elitist politics has been challenged. Shakespeare is decreasingly viewed as the exclusive property of certain guardians of high culture, to be reconstructed, reappraised within their narrowly designated limits. He is being restored to the common domain.

REVISION QUESTIONS

1. In what respect is Volumnia entitled to say of Coriolanus, 'Thou art my warrior:/I holp to frame thee' (V.iii.62–3)?

2. Discuss the paradox of Coriolanus, a traitor whose whole life centres on his integrity.

3. What is the play's contribution to the debate on war's place in human affairs?

4. 'Despite its political background, the play's crucial question becomes how it is possible to value and express love in a loveless world.' Discuss.

5. It has been claimed that Coriolanus fights not primarily for his society but for himself. Consider this claim and the implications it would have for our understanding of the character.

6. Discuss contention as a structural principle of the play.

7. Is *Coriolanus* about the conflict of private identity and social responsibility?

8. Discuss the dramatic relationship of the women in the play.

9. 'The plebeians only look mean and despicable if we are determined to view Coriolanus as heroic and noble.' Test the truth of this claim.

10. 'The key relationship is not that between Coriolanus and Volumnia, or Coriolanus and Aufidius, but Coriolanus and the plebs.' Discuss.

11. Would you agree that *Coriolanus* is a personal tragedy involving and precipitating a larger political tragedy?

12. Develop Brecht's thought that Coriolanus's 'switch from being the most Roman of the Romans to becoming their deadliest enemy is due precisely to the fact that he stays the same'.

APPENDIX:

SHAKESPEARE'S THEATRE

We should speak, as Muriel Bradbrook reminds us, not of the Elizabethan stage but of Elizabethan stages. Plays of Shakespeare were acted on tour, in the halls of mansions, one at least in Gray's Inn, frequently at Court, and after 1609 at the Blackfriars, a small, roofed theatre for those who could afford the price. But even after his Company acquired the Blackfriars, we know of no play of his not acted (unless, rather improbably, *Troilus* is an exception) for the general public at the Globe, or before 1599 at its predecessor, The Theatre, which, since the Globe was constructed from the same timbers, must have resembled it. Describing the Globe, we can claim therefore to be describing, in an acceptable sense, Shakespeare's theatre, the physical structure his plays were designed to fit. Even in the few probably written for a first performance elsewhere, adaptability to that structure would be in his mind.

For the facilities of the Globe we have evidence from the drawing of the Swan theatre (based on a sketch made by a visitor to London about 1596) which depicts the interior of another public theatre; the builder's contract for the Fortune theatre, which in certain respects (fortunately including the dimensions and position of the stage) was to copy the Globe; indications in the dramatic texts; comments, like Ben Jonson's on the throne let down from above by machinery; and eye-witness testimony to the number of spectators (in round figures, 3000) accommodated in the auditorium.

In communicating with the audience, the actor was favourably placed. Soliloquising at the centre of the front of the great platform, he was at the mid-point of the theatre, with no one among the spectators more than sixty feet away from him. That platform-stage (Figs I and II) was the most important feature for performance at the Globe. It had the audience – standing in the yard (10) and seated in the galleries (9) – on three sides of it. It was 43 feet wide, and 27$\frac{1}{2}$ feet from front to back. Raised (?5 feet) above the level of the yard, it had a trap-door (II.8) giving access to the space below it. The actors, with their equipment, occupied the 'tiring house' (attiring-house: 2) immediately at the back of the stage. The stage-direction 'within' means inside the tiring-house. Along its frontage, probably from the top of the second storey, juts out the canopy or 'Heavens', carried on two large pillars rising through the platform (6, 7) and sheltering the rear part of the stage, the rest of which, like the yard, was open to the sky. If the 'hut' (I.8), housing the machinery for descents, stood, as in the Swan drawing, above the 'Heavens', that covering must have had a trap-door, so that the descents could be made through it.

Descents are one illustration of the vertical dimension the dramatist could use to supplement the playing-area of the great platform. The other opportunities are provided by the tiring-housing frontage or facade. About this facade the evidence is not as complete or clear as we should like, so that Fig. I is in part conjectural. Two doors giving entry to the platform there certainly were (3). A third (4) is probable but not certain. When curtained, a door, most probably this one, would furnish what must be termed a discovery-space (II.5), not an inner stage (on which action in any depth would have been out of sight for a significant part of the audience). Usually no more than two actors were revealed (exceptionally, three), who often then moved out on to the platform. An example of this is Ferdinand and Miranda in *The Tempest* 'discovered' at chess, then seen on the platform speaking with their fathers. Similarly the gallery (I.5) was not an upper stage. Its use was not limited to the actors: sometimes it functioned as 'lords' rooms' for favoured spectators, sometimes, perhaps, as a musicians' gallery. Frequently the whole gallery would not be needed for what took place aloft: a window-stage (as in the first balcony scene in *Romeo*, even perhaps in the second) would suffice. Most probably this would be a part (at one end) of the gallery itself; or just possibly, if the gallery did not (as it does in the Swan drawing) extend the whole width of the tiring-house, a window over the left or right-hand door. As the texts show, whatever was presented aloft, or in the discovery-space, was directly related to the action on the platform, so that at no time was there left, between the audience and the action of the drama, a great bare space of platform-stage. In relating Shakespeare's drama to the physical conditions of the theatre, the primacy of that platform is never to be forgotten.

Note: The present brief account owes most to C. Walter Hodges, *The Globe Restored*; Richard Hosley in *A new Companion to Shakespeare Studies*, and in *The Revels History of English Drama*; and to articles by Hosley and Richard Southern in *Shakespeare Survey*, 12, 1959, where full discussion can be found.

HAROLD BROOKS

SHAKESPEARE'S THEATRE

The stage and its adjuncts; the tiring-house; and the auditorium.

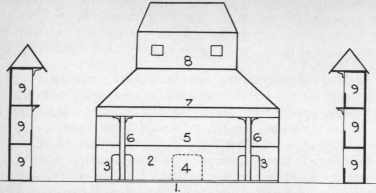

FIG I ELEVATION

1. Platform stage (approximately five feet above the ground) 2. Tiring-house
3. Tiring-house doors to stage 4. Conjectured third door 5. Tiring-house
gallery (balustrade and partitioning not shown) 6. Pillars supporting the
heavens 7. The heavens 8. The hut 9. The spectators' galleries

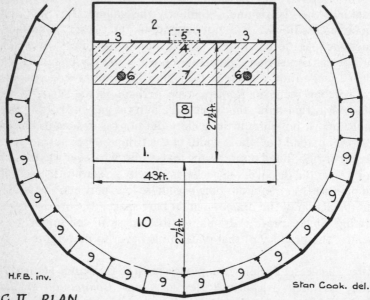

H.F.B. inv.

Stan Cook. del.

FIG II PLAN

1. Platform stage 2. Tiring-house 3. Tiring-house doors to stage
4. Conjectural third door 5. Conjectural discovery space (alternatively behind 3)
6. Pillars supporting the heavens 7. The heavens 8. Trap door 9. Spectators'
gallery 10. The yard

The Globe

An artist's imaginative recreation of a typical Elizabethan theatre

FURTHER READING

Bayley, John, 'The Thing I am. *Coriolanus*', *Shakespeare and Tragedy* (London: Routledge & Kegan Paul, 1981).

Berry, Ralph, 'The Metamorphoses of *Coriolanus*', *Changing Styles in Shakespeare*, (London: Allen & Unwin, 1981).

Bradley, A. C., '*Coriolanus*', *A Miscellany* (London: Macmillan, 1929).

Brecht, Bertolt, 'Study of the First Scene of Shakespeare's "Coriolanus"', *Brecht on Theatre*, edited and translated by John Willett (London:Methuen/New York: Hill & Wang, 1964).

Doran, Madeleine, 'The Language of Contention in *Coriolanus*', *Shakespeare's Dramatic Language* (London/Wisconsin: University of Wisconsin Press, 1976).

Granville-Barker, Harley, *Prefaces to Shakespeare. Fifth series: Coriolanus* (London: Sidgwick and Jackson, 1947).

Levin, Harry, 'An Introduction to *Coriolanus*', *Shakespeare and the Revolution of the Times* (New York: Oxford University Press, 1976).

MacCallum, M. W., *Shakespeare's Roman Plays and Their Background* (London: Macmillan, 1967; first published 1910).

Murry, John Middleton, 'A Neglected Heroine of Shakespeare', *Countries of the Mind* (London: Oxford University Press, 1922).

Palmer, John, *Political Characters of Shakespeare* (London: Macmillan, 1945).

Shakespeare Survey and *Shakespeare Quarterly* are valuable sources. See especially vol. 10 (1957) of the former, which is devoted to the Roman plays. In the latter, J. R. Mulryne, '*Coriolanus* at Stratford-upon-Avon: Three Actors' Remarks', 29 (1978) is especially stimulating.

Essays in Criticism has an interesting group of related articles: D. J. Enright, '*Coriolanus*. Tragedy or Debate?', 4 (1954); Kenneth Muir, 'In Defence of the Tribunes', 4 (1954); and I. R. Browning, '*Coriolanus*: Boy of Tears', 5 (1955).